RADICAL
Forgiveness
Making Room for the Miracle

By COLIN C.TIPPING

2nd Edition

Copyright © 2002, Colin C.Tipping.

RADICAL Forgiveness, Making Room for the Miracle.

First Published in October, 1997
> *Second Printing, June, 1998*
> *Third Printing, June, 1999*
> *Fourth Printing, November, 2000*

Library of Congress   97-074058

Second Edition: Published in Spring, 2002

RADICAL Forgiveness, Radical Forgiveness Therapy (RFT), and 'Satori' Breathwork are Trademarks of Global 13 Company Trust and the Institute of Radical Forgiveness Therapy and Coaching, Inc.

ISBN 0-9704814-1-1

Global 13 Publications, Inc.
26 Briar Gate Lane,
Marietta GA 30066
sales@radicalforgiveness.com
Website: www.radicalforgiveness.com
Cover Design: Fragile Design, Melbourne, Australia.
Illustrations: JoAnna Tipping
Editing: Nina Amir Lacey & Elizabeth Grobes
Proof Reading: Diana Urbas

Disclaimer: *Though the reader may observe some similarities between Radical Forgiveness and A Course in Miracles, I wish to make it clear that, although I am familiar with some of the principles taught in ACIM, I have never been either a student or a teacher of it and therefore this is not in any sense an ACIM Book. C.T.*

Praise For This Book:

CAROLINE MYSS, Ph.D. — *author of "Anatomy of the Spirit" & 'Why People Don't Heal and How They Can"*

"I LOVE this book! We can never say enough about the significance of forgiveness, nor offer people – ourselves especially, enough guidance on how to accomplish this arduous task."

NEALE DONALD WALSCH — *Author of the "Conversations With God" series.*

" This is the most exciting book on forgiveness to come out in a very long time. I have never seen anything so well written, so clearly articulated, so remarkably cohesive and so right on the money on this topic. I am recommending Radical Forgiveness to everyone. It is a book that can change - and save - people's lives. For some it will be a gift of a lifetime."

JOHN BRADSHAW — *PBS Broadcaster, lecturer, and author of "Healing the Shame That Binds You," "Homecoming," "Creating Love," and "Family Secrets."*

"Anger work that does not take us towards forgiveness becomes just another addiction. This superb book gives us the tools that makes genuine forgiveness possible, enabling us to really move beyond our pain and heal our lives."

JEFF GATES — *Author of "The Ownership Solution," and a consultant to the U.S. Government and governments worldwide.*

"The healing now needed in the world is not limited to individuals; it extends to nations, corporations and institutions. Yet the way forward has been blocked for the want of tools required for effective atonement, apology and forgiveness. Colin Tipping, a brilliant pioneer in this fast-emerging area, provides just the sort of transformational tools required if we are to leave for our children a more peaceful and harmonious world."

C. NORMAN SHEALY, M.D. Ph.D.— *Co-author with Caroline Myss of "The Creation of Health."*

"Radical Forgiveness — What a critically important concept and useful approach!"

ALAN COHEN — *best selling author of "The Dragon Doesn't Live Here any More," and "I Had It All the time."*

"The book is magnificent and I am proud to endorse it wholeheartedly. Radical Forgiveness is a masterfully presented system of undoing what has caused pain in people's lives. My hat's off to Colin Tipping for joining heart and mind to bring illumination to a most important area. Practice these dynamic principles and your life will become new!"

CATHERINE PONDER. *Unity Church Worldwide. Author of "The Dynamic Laws of Prosperity" and "The Dynamic Laws of Healing."*

"I receive so many requests to endorse books that I have a "no endorsement" policy. But this one on forgiveness is so needed, that I am making an exception in this case. My readers write me of the most amazing experiences they have from practicing daily the miracle power of forgiveness. Try forgiveness for yourself, regularly and consistently, and feel the power of relief and release from burdensome hurts; then make way for whatever miracles you need next in your life! This book shows you how!

MARK VICTOR HANSON — *author of "Chicken Soup for the Soul," and many other books.*

"Colin teaches and writes about the only truly effortless way to achieve forgiveness that I have ever experienced. I love his book, his seminars and the methods he gives us to process all our forgiveness needs without friction, pain, resentment or resistance."

(Mark and his wife attended a Circles of Forgiveness workshop in Costa Mesa, CA., June 30, 2002.)

iv

Dedicated to the Memory of
Diana, Princess of Wales,
who through her demonstration of the transforming
power of love, opened the heart chakra of
Great Britain and much of the world.

Acknowledgements

My gratitude and love goes first to my wife, JoAnna, for believing in me and giving me total support for writing this book, even when times got hard. I also owe a special debt of gratitude to my sister Jill, and brother-in-law, Jeff, for allowing me to publish a very personal story about them both, without which this book would have been very much impoverished. I also acknowledge Jeff's daughter Lorraine and my daughter Lorraine for the same reason and all the members of Jill's and Jeff's family who were willing to read the book and to see the best in each person who had a part to play in Jill's story. I also acknowledge my brother John who witnessed the unfolding of the story, for his patience and support. I owe a special debt of gratitude to Michael Ryce for his inspiration on the forgiveness worksheets and to Arnold Patent for introducing me to spiritual law. There are countless numbers who have contributed in very important ways to this book and to the work of spreading the message of Radical Forgiveness and I give thanks daily for every one of them. Thanks are due to all my Graduates of the Institute of Radical Forgiveness who are living it and doing it by example and as teachers. Special thanks to Debi Lee for letting me tell her story around the world and to Karen Taylor-Good whose songs and singing add an indescribably wonderful tone to every workshop I do — especially when she's there in person. Special appreciation is due to my co-workers and colleagues at the Institute for Radical Forgiveness Therapy and Coaching, Inc., — Pamela Black, Patrick O'Rourke, Neil Wheatley and Sandra Richmond. My thanks also to Elizabeth Grobes for her careful final edit and to Diana Urbas and Cecilia Rinaldi for proof reading. I wish to express a special appreciation for Brian Copping who has helped me extend and refine my thinking and with whom I am now creating an exciting new future, along with Karen Bates who has also just recently joined the team. Thanks are also due to C.J. Ryce and Ryan Malham for creating a fantastic, interactive web site and to Deborah Hill for all her graphic art expertise and help. Finally, my love and gratitude to my mother and my father for choosing to have me and for accepting my request to incarnate through them.

Foreword

When I was a student at London University I had the rare opportunity to attend a lecture given by a professor of great standing whose writings on the Philosophy of Education were legendary. After the lecture, a student stood up and challenged the professor, saying that something in his lecture contradicted what he had written in his book. I was flabbergasted by the professor's response. He said, *"Oh yes, I did say that in my book, but I've changed my mind since then. I no longer hold that to be true."* I almost fell off my chair. I realized in that moment that, until then, I had always considered anything in print to be, if not the absolute truth, at the very least the immutable and definitive opinion of the author. The fact that this revered figure could disagree with his own book was both a shock and a revelation to me.

The great advantage I have over my professor, however, is that, since I am my own publisher, I can keep my book current with my thinking any time I do a new print run by adding, deleting and changing any part of it. Don't worry though—I can assure you that I have not changed my mind about Radical Forgiveness.

Though most people won't have noticed, I have made incremental changes in the book at almost every printing. In 2002 I made sufficient changes and additions to warrant coming out with it as an official second edition. It had a brand new and much improved cover, to which everyone responded very favorably. I re-wrote some chapters, added others and modified the worksheet quite considerably—to make it easier to use. I also added an Epilogue dealing with the 911 event. It went from 288 pages to 320 without any increase in price.

At the same time as coming out with the second edition, I introduced a new Radical Forgiveness tool on CD called The 13 Steps to Radical Forgiveness. *(See the inside back cover)*.

This CD is complementary to the book in that it is, in effect, an audio worksheet. The same kind of things that are on the worksheet are spoken on the CD, except that they are framed as 13 questions to which the answer to each of them is, 'Yes.' It is deceptively simple but incredibly potent. Belief is not necessary—you just play the track, say 'Yes' 13 times and the same kind of miracles occur as with the worksheet. It's unbelievable! And it only takes about five minutes to do.

The CD also has on it four wonderful songs by my favorite musician, Karen Taylor-Good. Her songs are clearly aligned with Radical Forgiveness and her rendering of them really quite lovely. *(See last page in this book)*.

With this latest printing in 2003, the only significant change I have made, besides updating the Appendices and replacing the Epilogue on 9/11 with an Afterword, is to replace Chapter 30, *The Wake For the Inner Child* with a chapter on *Radical Self-Forgiveness*. (The 'Wake' meditation remains available on CD and tape).

In the second edition, I had made the mistake of promising a forthcoming book on Self-Forgiveness. When I made a start on it, I realized that it would be almost identical to this book, the main difference being only that I would simply be swapping the word *victim* for *perpetrator*. Nevertheless, I have been doing self-forgiveness workshops this year and have used what I have learned in doing those to craft a very interesting chapter on the subject of self-forgiveness. I have also decided, instead of writing a book, to create an on-line program that will be more effective. *(See Appendix 1, page 295)*

The Epilogue on 9/11, which was a demonstration of how the Four Steps to Radical Forgiveness process can be used in situations like 9/11, is now archived on our web site and can be downloaded at no charge. At the Home page, click on *'America's Healing.'* You will find it there.

As with this Foreword, change is the theme of the Afterword. *(See pages 283- 290).* But, whereas what you are reading now is about where we are at present, the Afterword sets out my vision for where we are going with Radical Forgiveness. I have placed it at the end of the book because it will be much more meaningful to you once you have read the intervening pages and done a few worksheets.

*(**Note:** To read this book and not do the worksheets is to completely miss the point. Radical Forgiveness has to be experienced to be appreciated — it is not an intellectual exercise — and the worksheet is what the book is all about. So don't shortchange yourself by not doing at least a few worksheets to straighten out some of the kinks in the hose*

that keep your energy blocked. Your life will work better and you might even have some miracles show up in your life. You deserve it, surely.)

I have also written and published a new book which is entitled, **A Radical Incarnation.** *(See Appendix III, Page 306 and 307).* It is a very unusual book in that it seeks to explain, in spiritual terms, what is going on in the world today. The subtitle is ***The President of the U.S. Becomes Enlightened, Heals America and Awakens Humanity - A Spiritual Fantasy.***

Yes, it is quite funny, but it also has a very serious side to it. In 1999 I stated my mission thus: ***"My mission is to raise the consciousness of the planet through Radical Forgiveness and create a world of forgiveness by 2012."*** The Radical Incarnation book, and the on-line program associated with it, are testimony to the fact that I have finally come to believe that this is not just a dream, but that it is eminently possible. This book not only indicates how it might occur but also invites you to help make it happen.

Well, that's the news for now on current updates. Look out for another new book coming out in 2004 showing how Radical Forgiveness can be used in the workplace. In the meanwhile, read and enjoy this book, do some worksheets and then join me in the Afterword for a further conversation on what's next. By that time, you might have found yourself embarked upon the journey of a lifetime! I hope so, because I cannot do this alone. I need you and many others like you to bring the dream of a healed world into being.

Namaste.

Contents

ILLUSTRATIONS & TABLES

Introduction

Everywhere we look — in the newspapers, TV, and even in our own personal lives, we see examples of egregiously hurt victims. We read, for example, that at least one out of every five adults in America today was either physically or sexually abused as a child. TV news confirms that rape and murder is commonplace in our communities and crime against the person and property is rampant everywhere. Around the world we see torture, repression, incarceration, genocide and open warfare occurring on a vast scale.

Over a period of ten years, since I began doing forgiveness workshops, cancer retreats and corporate seminars, I have heard enough horror stories from quite ordinary people to convince me that there is not a human being on the planet that has not been seriously victimized at least once in their lifetime, and in minor ways more times than they could count. Who among us could say they have never blamed someone else for their lack of happiness? For most, if not all of us, that simply is a way of life.

Indeed, the victim archetype is deeply engrained in all of us, and exerts great power in the mass consciousness. For eons we have been playing out victimhood in every aspect of our lives, convincing ourselves that victim consciousness is absolutely fundamental to the human condition.

The time has come to ask ourselves the question — how can we stop creating our lives this way and let go of the victim archetype as the model of how to live our lives?

1

To break free from such a powerful archetype, we must replace it with something *radically* different — something so compelling and spiritually liberating that it magnetizes us away from the victim archetype and the world of illusion. We need something that will take us beyond the drama of our lives so we can see the big picture and the *truth* that, right now, lies hidden from us. When we awaken to that truth, we will understand the true meaning of our suffering and be able to transform it immediately.

As we move into the new millenium and prepare for the imminent next great leap in our spiritual evolution, it is essential that we adopt a way of living based not on fear, control and abuse of power, but on true forgiveness, unconditional love and peace. That's what I mean by something *radical*, and that is what my book is all about — helping us make that transition.

To transform anything, we must be able to experience it completely and fully, which means that to transform the victim archetype, we must experience victimhood fully. There is no short cut! Therefore, we need situations in our lives that allow us to feel victimized so we can transform the energy through **Radical Forgiveness.**

To transform an energy pattern so fundamental as the victim archetype, many, many souls must accept this as their spiritual mission — souls who possess the wisdom and love necessary to accomplish this immense task. Perhaps you are one of the souls who volunteered for this mission. Could that be why this book speaks to you?

Jesus gave a powerful demonstration of what transforming the victim archetype means and I believe he now waits patiently and lovingly for us to follow his lead. Up to now at least, we have failed to learn from his example precisely because the victim archetype has had such a strong hold in our psyche.

We have ignored the lesson of genuine forgiveness that Jesus taught — that there are no victims. Yet, we straddle the fence and attempt to forgive while staying firmly committed to being a victim. We have made Jesus the ultimate victim. This will not move us forward in our spiritual evolution. True forgiveness must include letting go completely of victim consciousness.

Indeed, my main intention in writing this book was to make clear the distinction between forgiveness that maintains the victim archetype and **Radical Forgiveness** that frees us from it. Radical Forgiveness challenges us to radically shift our perception of the world and our interpretations of what happens to us in our lives so we can stop being a victim. My one goal is to help you make that shift.

I recognize that the ideas I am presenting here might be extremely challenging for someone severely victimized and still carrying a lot of pain. I ask only that you read this book with an open mind and see whether or not you feel better after reading it.

As I write this second edition of the book I can tell you that the feedback I have been getting from my readers and from those who come to my workshops is overwhelmingly positive. Even people who have been in emotional pain for a long time have found the book to be extremely freeing and healing — and the workshops transformational.

What has also been amazing and gratifying is the extent to which Chapter One, *'Jill's Story,'* has created instant healing for many, many people. I originally thought I was writing it as a useful lead-in to the concepts and ideas about Radical Forgiveness, but I now recognize that Spirit knew better and was guiding my hand all the way on this. I get many phone calls from people, often still in tears, who, having just read the story, tell me that they see themselves in it and feel that their healing has already begun.

A great many of these have been moved to share their experience with others by E-mailing *'Jill's Story'* directly from my website* to all their friends, relations and business associates — a wonderful chain reaction!

I shall be forever grateful to my sister and brother-in-law for allowing me to tell their story and for making that gift to the world.

I find myself very humbled by the overall response I am getting to the book and it is fast becoming clear to me that I am being used by Spirit to get this message out so that we can all heal, raise our vibration and go home. I am grateful to be of service.

Namaste

Colin Tipping

PART ONE
A Radical Healing

Author's Note

*T*o give you, the reader, an understanding of what I call Radical Forgiveness, I have presented the following true account of how this process saved my sister's marriage and changed her life. Since that time, Radical Forgiveness has positively impacted the lives of countless others, for not long after this episode with my sister, I realized that the process could be used as a form of help quite different from traditional psychotherapy and relationship counseling. I now offer what I call Radical Forgiveness Coaching to clients in my private practice and in my workshops, and seldom need to do the kind of therapy I once did. This is because I find that problems more or less disappear when you teach people how to use the tools of Radical Forgiveness.

C.T.

1: Jill's Story

As soon as I saw my sister, Jill, emerge into the lobby of Atlanta's Hartsfield International Airport, I knew something was wrong. She had never hidden her feelings well, and it was apparent to me that she was in emotional pain.

Jill had flown from England to the United States with my brother John, whom I had not seen for sixteen years. He emigrated from England to Australia in 1972 and I to America in 1984 — thus Jill was, and still is, the only one of the three siblings living in England. John had made a trip home, and this trip to Atlanta represented the last leg of his return journey. Jill accompanied him to Atlanta so she could visit me and my wife, JoAnna, for a couple of weeks and see him off to Australia from there.

After the initial hugging and kissing and a certain amount of awkwardness, we set out for the hotel. I had arranged rooms for one night so JoAnna and I could show them Atlanta the next day before driving north to our home.

As soon as the first opportunity for serious discussion presented itself, Jill said, "Colin, things are not good at home. Jeff and I might be splitting up."

Despite the fact that I had noticed that something seemed wrong with my sister, this announcement surprised me. I had always thought she and her husband, Jeff, were happy in their six-year-old marriage. Both had been married before, but this relationship had seemed strong. Jeff had three kids with his previous wife, while Jill had four. Her youngest son, Paul, was the only one still living at home.

"What's going on?" I asked.

"Well, it's all quite bizarre and I don't quite know where to begin," she replied. "Jeff is acting really strange and I can't stand much more of it. We've gotten to the point where we can't talk to each other anymore. It's killing me. He has totally turned away from me and says that it's all my fault."

"Tell me about it," I said, glancing at John, who responded by rolling his eyes. He'd stayed at their house for a week prior to flying to Atlanta, and I guessed by his demeanor that he'd heard enough of this subject to last him a while.

"Do you remember Jeff's eldest daughter, Lorraine?" Jill asked. I nodded. "Well, her husband got killed in a car crash about a year ago. Ever since then, she and Jeff have developed this really weird relationship. Any time she calls, he fawns over her, calling her *'Love,'* and spending hours talking to her in hushed tones. You'd think they were lovers — not father and daughter. If he's in the middle of something and she calls, he drops everything to talk with her. If she comes to our home, he acts just the same — if not worse. They huddle together in this deep and hushed conversation that excludes everyone else — especially me. I can hardly stand it. I feel she has become the center of his life, and I hardly figure in at all. I feel totally shut out and ignored."

She went on and on, offering more details of the strange family dynamic that had developed. JoAnna and I listened attentively. We wondered aloud about the cause of Jeff's behavior and were generally sympathetic. We made suggestions as to how she might talk to him about his behavior and generally struggled to find a way to fix things, as would any concerned brother and sister-in-law. John was supportive and offered his perspective on the situation as well.

What seemed strange and suspicious to me was the uncharacteristic nature of Jeff's behavior. The Jeff I knew was affectionate with his daughters and certainly co-dependent enough to badly need their approval and love, but I had never seen him behave in the manner Jill described. I had always known him as caring and affectionate towards Jill. In fact, I found it hard to believe that he would treat her quite so cruelly. I found it easy to understand why this situation made Jill unhappy and how Jeff's insistence that she was imagining it all and making herself mentally ill over it, made it all so much worse for her.

The conversation continued all the next day. I began to get a picture of what might be going on between Jill and Jeff from a Radical Forgiveness standpoint, but decided not to mention it — at least not right away. She was too

9

caught up in the drama of the situation and wouldn't have been able to hear and understand what I had to say. Radical Forgiveness is based on a very broad spiritual perspective that was not our shared reality when we were all still living in England. Feeling certain that both she and John were unaware of my beliefs underlying Radical Forgiveness, I felt the time had not yet arrived to introduce so challenging a thought as *this is perfect just the way it is — and an opportunity to heal.*

However, after the second day of verbally going round and round about the problem, I decided the time was near for me to try the Radical Forgiveness approach. This would require that my sister open up to the possibility that something beyond the obvious was happening — something that was purposeful, divinely guided and intended for her highest good. Yet, she was so committed to being the *victim* in the situation, I wasn't sure I could get her to hear an interpretation of Jeff's behavior that would take her out of that role.

However, just as my sister began yet another repetition of what she had said the day before, I decided to intervene. Tentatively, I said, "Jill, are you willing to look at this situation differently? Would you be open to me giving you a quite different interpretation of what is happening?"

She looked at me quizzically, as if she were wondering, *'How can there possibly be another interpretation? It is how it is!'* However, I have a certain track record with Jill in that I had helped her solve a relationship problem before, so she trusted me enough to say, "Well, I guess so. What do you have in mind?"

This was the opening I was waiting for. "What I'm going to say may sound strange, but try not to question it until I have finished. Just stay open to the possibility that what I am saying is true, and see whether or not what I say makes sense to you in any way at all."

Until this time, John had done his best to stay attentive to Jill, but the constant repetitive conversation about Jeff had begun to bore him tremendously. In fact, he had largely tuned her out. However, I was acutely aware that my interjection caused John to perk up and begin listening again.

"What you have described to us, Jill, certainly represents the truth as you see it," I began. "I have not the slightest doubt in my mind that this is occurring just as you say it is. Besides, John has witnessed much of the situation over the last three weeks and confirms your story, right John?" I queried, turning toward my brother.

"Absolutely," he confirmed. "I saw it going on a lot, just as Jill says. I thought it was pretty strange and, quite honestly, much of the time I felt awkward being there."

"I'm not surprised," I said. "Anyway Jill, I want you to know that nothing I am going to say negates what you have said or invalidates your story. I believe that it happened the way you said it happened. Let me, however, give you a hint of what might be going on underneath this situation."

11

"What do you mean, *underneath the situation,*" Jill asked, eyeing me suspiciously.

"It's perfectly natural to think that everything *out there* is *all* there is to reality," I explained. "But maybe there's a whole lot more happening beneath that reality. We don't perceive anything else going on because our five senses are inadequate to the task. But that doesn't mean it isn't occurring.

"Take your situation. You and Jeff have this drama going on. That much is clear. What if, beneath the drama, something of a more spiritual nature was happening — same people and same events — but a totally different meaning? What if your two souls were doing the same dance but to a wholly different tune? What if the dance was about you healing? What if you could see this as an opportunity to heal and grow? That would be a very different interpretation, would it not?"

Both she and John looked at me as if I were now speaking a foreign language. I decided to back off from the explanation and to go directly for the experience.

"Looking back over the last three months or so Jill," I went on. "What did you feel mostly when you saw Jeff behaving so lovingly towards his daughter, Lorraine?"

"Anger mostly," she said, but continued thinking about it. "Frustration," she added. Then, after a long pause, "and sadness. I really feel sad." Tears welled up in her eyes. "I feel so alone and unloved," she said and began sobbing quietly. "It wouldn't be so bad if I thought he couldn't show love, but he can and he does — but with *her!*"

She spat the last few words out with vehemence and rage and began to sob uncontrollably for the first time since her arrival. She'd shed a few tears prior to this, but she hadn't really let herself cry. Now, at last, she was letting go. I was pleased that Jill had been able to get in touch with her emotions that quickly.

A full 10 minutes went by before her crying subsided and I felt she could talk. At that point, I asked, "Jill, can you ever remember feeling this same way when you were a little girl?" Without the slightest hesitation, she said, "Yes." She was not immediately forthcoming about when, so I asked her to explain. It took her a while to respond.

"Dad wouldn't love me either!" she blurted out finally and began to sob again. "I wanted him to love me, but he wouldn't. I thought he couldn't love anyone! Then your daughter came along, Colin. He loved her all right. So why couldn't he love me, God damnit?!" She banged her fist hard on the table as she shouted the words and dissolved into more uncontrollable tears.

Jill's reference was to my eldest daughter, Lorraine. Coincidentally, or rather, synchronistically, she and Jeff's eldest daughter had the same name.

Crying felt really good to Jill. Her tears served as a powerful release and possibly a turning point for her. A real breakthrough might not be far away, I thought. I needed to keep nudging her forward.

"Tell me about the incident with my daughter, Lorraine, and Dad," I said.

"Well," Jill said, while composing herself. "I always felt unloved by Dad and really craved his love. He never held my hand or sat me on his lap much. I always felt there must be something wrong with me. When I was older, Mom told me she didn't think Dad was capable of loving anyone, not even her. At that time I, more or less, made peace with that. I rationalized that if he wasn't really capable of loving anyone, then it wasn't my fault that he didn't love me. He really didn't love anyone. He hardly ever made a fuss of my kids — his own grandchildren — much less people or kids not his own. He was not a bad father. He just couldn't love. I felt sorry for him."

She cried some more, taking her time now. I knew what she meant about our father. He was a kind and gentle man but very quiet and withdrawn. For the most part, he certainly had seemed emotionally unavailable to anyone.

As Jill became more composed once again, she continued, "I remember a particular day at your house. Your daughter Lorraine was probably about four or five years old. Mom and Dad were visiting from Leicester, and we all came to your house. I saw your Lorraine take Dad's hand. She said, *'Come on, Grandad. Let me show you the garden and all my flowers.'* He was like putty in her hands. She

14

led him everywhere and talked and talked and talked, showing him all the flowers. She enchanted him. I watched them out of the window the whole time. When they came back in, he put her on his lap and was as playful and joyful as I have ever seen him.

"I was devastated. *'So, he is able to love after all,'* I thought. If he could love Lorraine, then why not me?" The last few words came out as a whisper followed by deep long tears of grief and sadness, tears held in for all those years.

I figured we had done enough for the time being, and suggested we make tea. *(Well, we're English! We always make tea, no matter what!)*

Interpreting Jill's story from a Radical Forgiveness standpoint, I easily saw that Jeff's outwardly strange behavior was unconsciously designed to support Jill in healing her unresolved relationship with her father. If she could see this and recognize the perfection in Jeff's behavior, she could heal her pain — and Jeff's behavior would almost certainly stop. However, I wasn't sure how to explain this to Jill in a way she could understand at this point in time. Luckily, I didn't have to try. She stumbled on the obvious connection by herself.

Later that day she asked me, "Colin, don't you think it's odd that Jeff's daughter and your daughter both have the same name? Come to think of it, both of them are blonde and first born. Isn't that a strange coincidence! Do you think there's a connection?"

15

I laughed, and replied, "Absolutely. It's the key to under-standing this whole situation."

She looked at me long and hard. "What do you mean?"

"Work it out for yourself," I replied. "What other similari-ties do you see between that situation with Dad and my Lorraine, and your current situation?"

"Well, let's see," said Jill. "Both girls have the same name. Both of them were getting what I don't seem to be able to get from the men in my life."

"What?" I enquired.

"Love," she said in a whisper.

"Go on," I urged gently.

"It seems that your Lorraine was able to get the love from Dad that I couldn't. And Jeff's daughter, Lorraine, gets all the love she wants from her Dad, but at my expense. Oh, my God!" she exclaimed. She really was beginning to understand now.

"But why? I don't understand why. It's a bit frightening! What the heck's going on?" she asked in a panic.

It was time to put the pieces together for her. "Look, Jill," I said. "Let me explain how this works. This happens to be a perfect example of what I was talking about earlier when I said that beneath the drama we call life lies a whole different reality. Believe me, there's nothing to be frightened about. When you see how this works, you will feel more trust, more security and more peace than you ever thought possible. You'll realize how well we are being supported by the Universe or God, whatever you want to call it, every moment of every day no matter how bad any given situation seems at the time," I said as reassuringly as I could.

"Looked at from a spiritual standpoint, our discomfort in any given situation provides a signal that we are out of alignment with spiritual law and are being given an opportunity to heal something. It may be some original pain or perhaps a toxic belief that stops us from becoming our true selves. We don't often see it from this perspective, however. Rather, we judge the situation and blame others for what is happening, which prevents us from seeing the message or understanding the lesson. This prevents us from healing. If we don't heal whatever needs to be healed, we must create more discomfort until we are literally forced to ask, *'What is going on here?'* Sometimes the message has to become very loud, or the pain extremely intense, before we pay attention. A life threatening illness, for example, provides a loud message. Yet, even when facing death some people don't get the connection between what is happening in their lives and the opportunity for healing that it provides.

"In your case, what has come up to be healed this time is your original pain around your father and the fact that he never showed you love. That is what all your current pain

17

and discomfort is about. This particular pain has arisen many times before in different situations, but, because you didn't recognize the opportunity, it never got healed. That's why having yet another opportunity to look at and heal this issue is a gift!"

"A gift?" Jill questioned. "You mean it's a gift because there's a message in it for me? One that I might have gotten a long time ago if I'd been able to see it?"

"Yes," I said. "Had you seen it then, your discomfort would have been less and you wouldn't be going through this now. No matter. Now is fine, too. This is perfect, and you won't now have to produce a life-threatening illness to understand this, like so many people do. You're getting it now; you're beginning to understand and to heal.

"Let me explain to you exactly what happened and how it has effected your life up until now," I said, wanting her to understand clearly the dynamics of her current situation.

"As a little girl, you felt abandoned and unloved by Dad. For a girl, this is devastating. From a developmental standpoint, it is necessary for a young girl to feel loved by her father. Since you didn't feel that love, you concluded that there must something wrong with you. You began to really believe you were unlovable and inherently *not enough*. That belief anchored itself deeply in your subconscious mind and, later, when it came to relationships, began to run your life. In other words, as a way of mirroring your subconscious belief that you were *not enough*, your life always has included actual situations exhibiting to you the fact that you were, indeed, not enough. Life will always prove your beliefs right.

"As a child, the pain of not getting Dad's love was more than you could bear, so you suppressed some of the pain and repressed a whole lot more. When you suppress emotion, you know its there, but you stuff it down. Repressed emotion, on the other hand, gets buried so deeply in the subconscious mind that you lose awareness of it.

"Later, when you began to realize that your father was not a naturally loving man and probably couldn't love anyone, you began to somewhat rehabilitate or heal yourself from the affects of feeling unloved by him. You probably released some of the suppressed pain and maybe began to give up some part of the belief that you were unlovable. After all, if he couldn't love anyone, maybe it wasn't your fault that he didn't love you.

"Then, along comes the bombshell that knocked you right back to square one. When you observed him loving my Lorraine, that triggered your original belief. You said to yourself, *'My father can love after all, but he doesn't love me. It is obviously my fault. I am not enough for my father, and I will never be enough for any man.'* From that point on, you continually created situations in your life to support your belief that you are *not enough."*

"How have I done that?" Jill interrupted. "I don't see how I have created myself not being enough in my life."

19

"How was your relationship with Henry, your first husband?" I responded. She had been married to Henry, the father of her four children, for 15 years.

"Not bad in many respects, but he was so unfaithful. He was always looking for opportunities to have sex with other women, and I really hated that."

"Exactly. And, you saw him as the villain and you as the victim in that situation. However, the truth is, you attracted him into your life precisely because, at some level, you knew he would prove your belief about not being enough. By being unfaithful, he would support you in being right about yourself."

"Are you trying to say he was doing me a favor? I sure as heck don't buy that!" she said laughingly, but also with some not-too-well-disguised anger.

"Well, he certainly supported your belief, didn't he?" I replied. "You were so *not enough* that he always was on the lookout for other women, for *something more*. If he had done the opposite and consistently treated you as if you were totally enough by being faithful, you would have created some other drama in your life to prove your belief. Your belief about yourself, albeit a totally false one, made it impossible for you to be enough.

"By the same token, had you at that time changed your belief by healing your original pain around your father and changed your belief to *I am enough*, Henry would have immediately stopped propositioning your friends. If he hadn't, you would have felt perfectly happy to leave him and find someone else who would treat you as though you were enough. We always create our reality according to our beliefs. If you want to know what your beliefs are, look at what you have in your life. Life always reflects our beliefs."

Jill seemed a bit perplexed, so I decided to reiterate some of the points I had made. "Each time Henry cheated on you, he gave you the opportunity to heal your original pain around being unloved by Dad. He demonstrated, and acted out for you, your belief that you were never going to be enough for any man. The first few times this happened, you may have gotten so mad and upset that you could have gotten in touch with the original pain and become acquainted with your belief system about yourself. In fact, his first acts of unfaithfulness represented your first opportunities to practice Radical Forgiveness and to heal your original pain, but you missed them. You made him wrong each time and created yourself as a victim instead, which made healing impossible."

"What do you mean forgiveness?" Jill asked, still looking troubled. "Are you saying I should have forgiven him for seducing my best friend and anyone else he could find who was willing?"

"I am saying that, at that time, he provided you with an opportunity to get in touch with your original pain and to see how a certain belief about yourself was running your

21

life. In so doing, he gave you the opportunity to understand and change your belief, thus healing your original pain. That's what I mean by forgiveness. Can you see why he deserves your forgiveness, Jill?"

"Yes, I think so," she said. "He was reflecting my belief— the one I had formed because I felt so unloved by Dad. He was making me right about not being enough. Is that correct?"

"Yes, and to the extent that he provided you with that opportunity, he deserves credit — actually, more than you realize right now. We have no way of knowing whether he would have stopped his behavior had you healed your issue around Dad at that time — or whether you would have left him. Either way, he would have served you powerfully well. So, in that sense, he deserves not only your forgiveness but your deep gratitude as well. And you know what? It wasn't his fault that you didn't understand the true message behind his behavior.

"I know that it was hard for you to see that he was trying to give you a great gift. That's not how we are taught to think. We're not taught to look at what is going on and to say, *'Look what I have created in my life? Isn't that interesting?'* Instead, we are taught to judge, lay blame, accuse, play victim and seek revenge. Neither are we taught to think that our lives are directed by forces other than our own conscious mind — but, in truth, they are.

22

"In fact, it was Henry's *soul* that tried to help you heal. On the surface, Henry just acted out his sexual addiction, but his soul — working with your soul — chose to use the addiction for your spiritual growth. Recognizing this fact is what Radical Forgiveness is all about. Its purpose lies in seeing the truth behind the apparent circumstances of a situation and recognizing the love that always exists there."

I felt that talking about her current situation would help Jill fully understand the principles I had described. So I said, "Let's take another look at Jeff and see how these principles are operating in your current relationship. In the beginning, Jeff was extremely loving towards you. He really doted on you, did things for you, communicated with you. On the surface, life with Jeff seemed pretty good.

"Remember, though, this didn't fit your picture of yourself — your belief about yourself. According to your belief, you shouldn't have a man who shows you this much love. You are not enough, remember?"

Jill nodded, but still looked uncertain and rather perplexed.

"Your soul knows you must heal that belief, so it colludes with Jeff's soul somehow to bring it to your awareness. On the surface it seems that Jeff begins to act strangely and totally out of character. He then taunts you by loving *another* Lorraine, thus acting out with you the very same scenario you had with your father many years ago. He appears to be persecuting you mercilessly, and you feel totally helpless and victimized. Does this describe, more or less, you current situation?" I asked.

23

"I guess so," Jill said quietly. She wrinkled her brow as she tried to hold on to the new picture of her situation slowly forming in her mind.

"Well, here you are again, Jill, about to make a choice. You must choose whether to heal and to grow — or to be right," I said and smiled.

"If you make the choice people normally make, you will choose to be the victim and make Jeff wrong, which in turn, allows you to be right. After all, his behavior seems quite cruel and unreasonable and I don't doubt there are many women who wouldn't support you in taking some drastic action in response to it. Haven't most of your friends been saying you should leave him?"

"Yes," she replied. "Everyone says I should get out of the marriage if he doesn't change. I actually thought that you would say that too," she said with a tinge of disappointment.

"A few years ago, I probably would have," I said and laughed. "However, since my introduction to these spiritual principles, my whole way of looking at such situations has changed, as you can see," I said with a wry smile, looking across at John. He grinned, but said nothing.

I continued. "So, as you might guess, the other choice might be to recognize that, beneath what seems to be happening on the surface, something else much more meaningful — and potentially very supportive — is going on. The other choice is to accept that Jeff's behavior may possess another message, another meaning, another intent, and that within the situation lies a gift for you."

Jill thought for a while, then said, "Jeff's behavior is so darn bizarre you'd have a hard time coming up with any good reason for it. Maybe something else is going on that I don't yet see. I suppose its similar to what Henry was doing, but it's hard for me to see it with Jeff, because I'm so confused right now. I can't see beyond what actually is going on."

"That's okay," I said reassuringly. "Look, there's no need to figure it out. Just being willing to entertain the idea that something else is going on is a giant step forward. In fact, the willingness to see the situation differently is the key to your healing. 90% of the healing occurs when you become willing to let in the idea that your soul has lovingly created this situation for you. In becoming willing, you let go of control and surrender it to God. He takes care of the other 10%. If you can really understand at a deep level and surrender to the idea that God will handle this for you if you turn it over to him, you won't need to do anything at all. The situation and your healing will both get handled automatically.

"However, prior even to this step, you can take a perfectly rational step that enables you to see things differently right away. It involves separating fact from fiction. It means recognizing that your belief has no factual basis whatsoever. It is simply a story you have made up, based on a few facts and a whole lot of interpretation.

25

"We do this all the time. We experience an event and make interpretations about it. Then, we put these two pieces together to create a largely false story about what happened. The story becomes the belief, and we defend it as if it were the truth. It never is, of course.

"In your case, the facts were that Dad didn't hug you, didn't spend time playing with you, didn't hold you, didn't put you on his lap. He did not meet your needs for affection. Those were the facts. On the basis of those facts, you made a crucial assumption: *'Dad doesn't love me.'* Isn't that true?" She nodded.

"However, the fact that he didn't meet your needs doesn't mean that he didn't love you. That's an interpretation. It wasn't true. He was a sexually repressed man and intimacy was scary for him; we know that. Maybe he just didn't know how to express his love in the way you wanted to receive it. Do you remember that super doll house he made you one year for Christmas? I remember him spending countless hours on it in the evenings when you were in bed. Perhaps that was the only way he knew how to express his love for you.

"I'm not making excuses for him or trying to make what you have said, or felt, wrong. I'm just trying to point out how we all make the mistake of thinking that our interpretations represent the truth.

"The next big assumption you made," I continued, "based on the facts *and* your first interpretation that *'Dad doesn't love me,'* was *'It's my fault. There must be something wrong with me.'* That was an even greater lie than the other assumption, don't you agree?" She nodded.

"It isn't surprising that you would come to that conclusion, because that's the way little kids think. Since they perceive that the world revolves around them, they always assume that when things don't go well, it's their fault. When a child first thinks this, the thought is coupled with great pain. To reduce the pain, a child represses it, but this action actually makes it all the harder to get rid of the thought. Thus, we stay stuck with the idea *'it's my fault and something must be wrong with me'* even as adults.

"Any time a situation in our life triggers the memory of this pain or the idea attached to it, we emotionally regress. Thus, we feel and behave like the little kid who first experienced the pain. In fact, that's precisely what happened when you saw my Lorraine cause our father to feel love. You were 27 years old, but at that moment you regressed to the two-year-old Jill who felt unloved and acted out all your childhood neediness. And you are still doing it, only this time you are doing it with your husband.

"The idea upon which you based all your relationships represents an interpretation made by a two-year-old kid and has absolutely no basis in fact," I concluded. "Do you see that, Jill?" I asked.

"Yes, I do," she replied. "I made some pretty silly decisions based on those unconscious assumptions, didn't I?"

27

"Yes, you did, but you made them when you were in pain and when you were too young to know any better. Even though you repressed the pain to get rid of it, the belief kept working in your life at a subconscious level. That's when your soul decided to create some drama in your life so you would bring it to consciousness again and have the opportunity to choose healing once more.

"You attracted people into your life who would confront you directly with your own pain and make you re-live the original experience through them," I continued.

"That's what Jeff is doing right now. Of course, I am not saying he is doing this consciously. He really isn't. He is probably more perplexed at his own behavior than are you. Remember, this is a soul-to-soul transaction. His soul knows about your original pain and is aware that you will not heal it without going through the experience again."

"Wow!" Jill said, and took a deep breath. She relaxed her body for the first time since we had begun talking about the situation.

"It's certainly a totally different way of looking at things, but do you know what? I feel lighter. It's as if a weight has been lifted off my shoulders just by talking it through with you."

"That's because your energy has shifted," I replied. "Imagine how much of your life-force energy you have had to expend just keeping the story about Dad and Lorraine alive. Plus, imagine the amount of energy required to keep down the feelings of grief and resentment wrapped around the story. The tears you shed earlier enabled you to release a lot of that. And you have just acknowledged that it was all just a made-up story anyway — what a relief that must be. In addition, you've had a lot of energy locked up around Jeff — making him wrong, making yourself wrong, being a victim, and so on. Just being willing to see the whole situation differently enables you to release all that energy and allow it to move through you. No wonder you feel lighter!" I said, and smiled.

"What would have happened if, instead of understanding what was going on underneath the situation with Jeff, I had simply left him?" Jill asked.

"Your soul would have brought in someone else to help you heal," I quickly replied. "But you didn't leave him, did you? You came here, instead. You have to understand, this trip was no accident. There are no such things as accidents in this system. You — or rather your soul — created this trip, this opportunity to understand the dynamics of the situation with Jeff. Your soul guided you here. John's soul created a trip at this particular time to make it possible for you to come with him."

"And what about the two Lorraines," Jill wondered. "How did that happen? Surely, that's just a coincidence."

"There are no coincidences in this system either. Just know that your souls, and the souls of some others, conspired to

29

create this situation, and notice how perfect it was that a person named Lorraine was involved in the original occasion and in this one. It couldn't have been a more perfect clue. It's hard to imagine that it wasn't set up somehow, don't you agree?" I said.

"So, what do I do with this now," asked Jill. "It's true that I feel lighter, but what do I do when I go home and see Jeff?"

"There really is very little for you to do," I answered. "From this point on, it's more a question of how you feel inside yourself. Do you understand that you are no longer a victim? Do you understand that Jeff is no longer a persecutor? Do you see that the situation was exactly what you needed and wanted? Do you feel how much that man loves you — at the soul level, I mean?"

"What do you mean?" Jill asked.

"He was willing to do whatever it took to get you to the point where you could look again at your belief about yourself and see that it was untrue. Do you realize how much discomfort he was willing to endure to help you? He is not a cruel man by nature, so it must have been hard for him. Few men could have done that for you while risking losing you in the process. Jeff, or Jeff's soul, truly is an angel for you. When you really understand this, you will feel so grateful to him! Plus, you will stop sending out messages that you are unlovable. You will have the ability to let in love perhaps for the first time in your life. You will have forgiven Jeff, because you will be clear that nothing wrong ever took place. It was perfect in every sense.

"And, I promise you this," I continued. "Jeff is already changing as we speak and dropping his bizarre behavior. His soul is already picking up that you have forgiven him and healed your misperception about yourself. As you change your energy, his changes too. You're connected energetically. Physical distance is irrelevant."

Getting back to her question, I said, "So, you won't have to do anything special when you get home. In fact, I want you to promise me that you won't do anything at all when you get back. In particular, do not, under any circumstances, share with Jeff this new way of looking at the situation. I want you to see how everything will be different automatically simply as a consequence of you changing your perception.

"You will feel changed as well," I added. "You will find yourself feeling more peaceful, more centered and more relaxed. You will have a knowingness that will seem strange to Jeff for a while. It will take time for your relationship with him to adjust, and it may still be difficult for a while, but this issue will resolve now," I concluded with conviction.

Jill and I reviewed this new way of looking at her situation many times before she returned home to England. It is always difficult for someone in the middle of an emotional upset to shift into a Radical Forgiveness perspective. In

31

fact, getting to a place where Radical Forgiveness can truly take place often requires a great deal of integration and repetitive reinforcement. To help my sister, I introduced her to some breathing techniques that help release emotion and integrate new ways of being and asked her to complete a Radical Forgiveness worksheet. (See Section Four, Tools For Radical Forgiveness.)

The day she left, Jill obviously was nervous about going back to the situation she had left behind. As she walked down the tunneled ramp to her airplane, she looked back and tried to wave confidently, but I knew she was scared that she might lose her newfound understanding and get drawn back into the drama.

Apparently the meeting with Jeff went well. Jill requested that he not question her immediately about what had happened while she was away. She also requested that he give her space for a few days in order to get settled. However, she immediately noticed a difference in him. He was attentive, kind and considerate — more like the Jeff she had known before this whole episode began.

Over the next couple of days, Jill told Jeff she no longer blamed him for anything, nor did she want him to change in any way. She said she had learned that it was she who needed to take responsibility for her own feelings and that she would deal with whatever came up for her in her own way without making him wrong. She did not elaborate at all and did not try to explain herself.

Things went on well for some days after Jill's return home, and Jeff's behavior with his daughter, Lorraine, changed dramatically. In fact, everything seemed to be getting back to normal with regard to that relationship, but the atmosphere between Jeff and Jill remained tense and their communication limited.

About two weeks later, the situation came to a head. Jill looked at Jeff and said quietly, "I feel like I've lost my best friend."

"So do I," he replied.

For the first time in months they connected. They hugged each other and began to cry. "Let's talk," Jill said. "I've got to tell you what I learned with Colin in America. It's going to sound weird to you at first, but I want to share it with you. You don't have to believe it. I just want you to hear me. Are you willing?"

"I'll do whatever it takes," replied Jeff. "I know something important happened to you there. I want to know what it was. You have changed and I like what I see. You are not the same person you were when you stepped on the airplane with John. So, tell me what happened."

Jill talked and talked. She explained the dynamics of Radical Forgiveness as best she could in a way Jeff could understand. She felt strong and powerful — sure of herself and her understanding, secure and clear in her mind.

33

Jeff, a practical man who always is skeptical of anything that cannot be rationally explained, did not resist this time — and was indeed quite receptive to the ideas that Jill asked him to consider. He voiced openness to the idea that there might be a spiritual world beneath everyday reality and, given that, saw a certain logic in the Radical Forgiveness concept. He didn't accept it totally, but he nevertheless was willing to listen, to consider and to see how it had changed Jill.

After the discussion, they both felt their love had been rekindled and that their relationship had a good chance of surviving. They made no promises, though, and agreed to keep talking to each other while they watched how their relationship progressed.

It did, indeed, progress quite well. Jeff still fawned over his daughter, Lorraine, to a degree, but not as much as before. Jill found she cared hardly at all, even when he did behave in this manner. It certainly did not trigger her to regress emotionally and react from old beliefs about herself.

Within a month of their conversation about Radical Forgiveness, all of Jeff's past behavioral pattern with Lorraine stopped. In turn, Lorraine didn't call or visit as often; she got on with her life. Everything slowly returned to normal and their relationship began to grow more secure and loving than ever before. Jeff became the kind, sensitive man that he is by nature, Jill became less needy and Lorraine became much happier.

Looking back, had Jill's soul not brought her to Atlanta to create the opportunity for us to have our conversation, I feel sure she and Jeff would have separated. In the grand scheme of things, that would have been all right, too. Jill simply would have found someone else with whom to rec-reate the drama and another opportunity to heal. As it was, she took the opportunity to heal this time, and stayed in the relationship.

At the time of writing this second edition, many years after that crisis, they remain together and are very happily mar-ried. Like every other couple they continue to create dra-mas in their lives — but they know now how to see them as healing opportunities and to move through them quickly and with grace.

Postscript: *The 'time-line' diagram on the next page depicts Jill's story as a graphic. She found this very helpful in seeing how the original pain of not feeling loved by her father had led to a belief that she was not enough and how, in turn, that belief had played out in her life. You might do the same for yourself if you think you have a similar story running your life.*

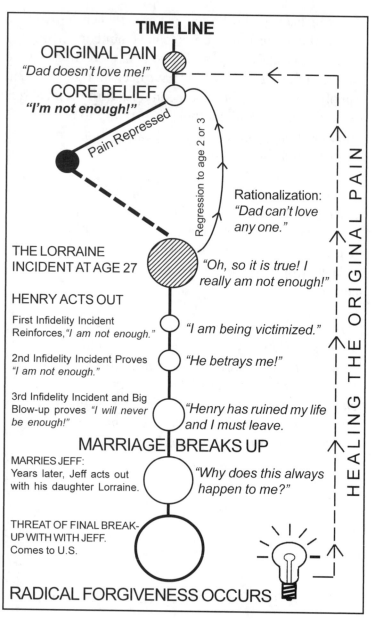

Fig. 1: Jill's Healing Journey

PART TWO

Conversations On Radical Forgiveness

2: Underlying Assumptions

Since all theories are based upon certain assumptions, it is important to have an understanding of the spiritual assumptions underlying the theory and practice of Radical Forgiveness.

Before looking at these though, it is worth noting that even the most widely accepted theories are based on assumptions for which there is very little hard evidence. For example, did you know that not one shred of evidence exists to support Darwin's Theory of Evolution? Historically, that theory probably ranks as one of the biggest assumptions ever made. It serves as the basic assumption behind all biological science and as the very foundation on which much of our accepted scientific *truth* rests. However, the fact that no evidence exists to prove this assumption true does not mean that the theory is invalid or not useful.

We can say the same thing about the basic assumptions handed down throughout the ages about God, human nature, and the spiritual realm. While there is little hard scientific evidence to support their validity, such assumptions have been handed down to us as *universal truths, or principles,* for centuries and have formed the foundation for many great spiritual traditions throughout the world. They certainly are foundational for Radical Forgiveness.

You will find in this chapter only brief and in some cases stark outlines of the assumptions underlying Radical Forgiveness. Nevertheless, they should be sufficient to help you follow the logic in the pages that immediately follow. Each assumption is expanded upon in length at various other places in the book.

Assumptions:

- Contrary to most Western religious thought, we are *not* human beings having an occasional spiritual experience; rather ***we are spiritual beings having a human experience.*** (An important and *radical* distinction!)
- We have bodies that die, but we have immortal souls that transcend death.
- While our bodies and our senses tell us we are separate individuals, we are all **one**. We all individually vibrate as part of a single whole.
- Vibrationally, we live in two worlds simultaneously:
  1) The World of Divine Truth
  2) The World of Humanity
- We have chosen to fully experience the energy of the World of Humanity in order to heal the wounds of our soul, especially the wound related to the idea that we are separated from God.
- When our spirits were one with God, we experimented with a thought that separation was possible.

We became trapped in that experiment, which became the illusion (sometimes called a dream), that we now live. It is an illusion because the separation did not happen. We only think it did. The belief that we are separate from God is what we are here to heal. It is the reason we are here.

- The Ego protects us from the overwhelming guilt that we felt when we imagined separation — as well as the fear of God's wrath — through the mechanisms of repression and projection. (See Chapter 7.)
- When we decided to experiment with physical incarnation (our way of separating), God gave us total **free will** to live this experiment in any way we chose and to find for ourselves the way back home.
- We come into the physical life experience with a mission — to fully experience a particular energy pattern so we can feel the feelings associated with that pattern and then transform that energy through love. (See Chapter 11).
- Life is not a random event. It is entirely purposeful and provides for the unfoldment of a divine plan with opportunities to make choices and decisions in every moment.
- We create our reality through the Law of Cause and Effect. Thoughts are causes that show up in our world as physical effects. Reality is an outplaying of our consciousness. Our world offers a mirror of our beliefs. (See Chapter 9.)
- We get precisely what we want in our lives. How we judge what we get determines whether we in fact experience life as either painful or joyful.

41

- Through relationship we grow and learn. Through relationship we heal and are returned to wholeness. We need others to mirror our misperceptions and our projections and to help us bring repressed material to consciousness for healing.
- Through the Law of Resonance, we attract people who resonate with our issues so we can heal them. For example, if abandonment is our issue, we will tend to attract people who abandon us. In that sense they serve as our teachers. (See Chapter 8).
- Physical reality is an illusion created by our five senses. Matter consists of interrelating energy fields vibrating at different frequencies. (See Chapter 13).

3: Worlds Apart

What we might learn from Jill's story is that things are not always what they seem. What appears to be cruel and nasty behavior on somebody's part might be exactly what we need and have indeed called forth. Situations that appear to be the worst that could possibly befall us may hold the key to our healing something deep within us that keeps us from being happy and prevents our growth. The people who seem to us to be the most troublesome and the least likeable could therefore be our greatest teachers.

If I am right about this, then it follows that whatever appears to be happening is seldom what is truly occurring. Beneath the apparent circumstances of every situation exists a wholly different reality — a different world altogether; a world that we are not privy to except for the occasional glimpse.

Jill's story demonstrates this fact beautifully. On the surface there was the drama of what was happening between her, Jeff and his daughter, Lorraine. It was not pretty. It looked as though Jeff was being cruel and insensitive. It was easy to identify Jill as a victim in the situation and Jeff as the villain. Yet there were enough clues in the situation to lead us to the possibility that something else of a more loving nature was happening — and that it was being orchestrated at the spiritual level.

As the story unfolded, it became obvious that Jill's soul was doing a dance with the souls of Jeff and Lorraine and that the situation being played out was purely for her healing. Moreover, far from being a villain, Jeff was actually a hero, and from that spiritual perspective, had done nothing wrong. He had simply played his part in the drama, as dictated by his soul, acting in support of Jill's healing at the soul level.

When we shift our perspective to this possibility, we become open to the idea that nothing wrong took place and that in fact there was nothing to forgive. This is precisely the notion that defines Radical Forgiveness. It is also what makes it RADICAL.

If we had asked Jill to apply traditional forgiveness to this situation, we would not have investigated this *'other world'* possibility. We would have taken the evidence of our five senses and used our intellect to come to the conclusion that she had been wronged and badly treated by Jeff and that if she was to forgive him she would have to accept what he did and try her best to let it go, or 'let bygones be bygones.'

From this we notice that traditional forgiveness takes it as a given that something wrong happened. Radical Forgiveness on the other hand takes the position that NOTHING wrong happened and that consequently, there is nothing to forgive. We can put it like this:

With **TRADITIONAL FORGIVENESS** *, the willingness to forgive is present but so is the residual need to condemn. Therefore victim consciousness is maintained and nothing changes.*

With **RADICAL FORGIVENESS** *, the willingness to forgive is present but NOT the need to condemn. Therefore the victim consciousness is dropped and everything changes.*

(**Victim Consciousness** is defined as the conviction that someone else has done something bad to you, and as a direct result, they are responsible for the lack of peace and happiness in your life).

Different Worlds — Different Perspectives

Traditional forgiveness should not be seen as being inferior to Radical Forgiveness. It is simply different. When used in the context of a certain set of beliefs — beliefs that are firmly rooted in the physical world and in everyday human reality, traditional forgiveness is the only form of forgiveness possible and has great value in its own right. It calls upon the finest of human qualities and characteristics, such as compassion, mercy, tolerance, humility and kindness. Joan Borysenko calls forgiveness "the exercise of compassion."*

---

* Guilt is the Teacher; Love is the Lesson," Warner Books, 1990

45

Radical Forgiveness is different from traditional forgiveness because it is rooted in the metaphysical reality of the world of Spirit — that which I call the World of Divine Truth.

This makes the distinction between Radical and traditional forgiveness very clear, because we can see now that in each case we look through completely different lenses. The lens we are using to view a situation through will determine whether we are using traditional forgiveness or Radical Forgiveness. Each one provides us with a totally different point of view.

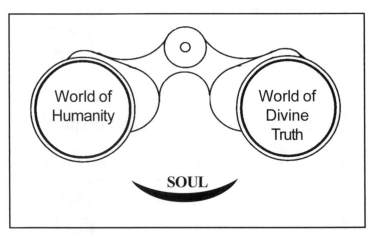

Figure 2: Perspectives On Two Worlds.

But we should not fall into the trap of thinking of it in terms of *either/or*. It is *a both/and* situation. This is because we live with one foot in each world (since we are spiritual beings having a human experience) and can therefore reference situations through either lens or both lenses at the same time. While being fully grounded in the World of Humanity, we remain connected to the World of Divine Truth through our soul.

Since the importance of the distinction between these two worlds cannot be overemphasized, some further explanation will be helpful here.

The World of Humanity and the World of Divine Truth represent two ends of a vibrational scale. When we vibrate at a low frequency, our bodies become dense and we exist only in the World of Humanity. When we vibrate at a high level, which makes our bodies become lighter, we exist also in the World of Divine Truth. Depending upon our vibration at any moment, we move up and down the scale toward one world or the other.

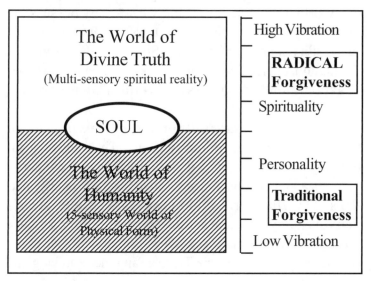

Figure 3. The Existential Chain of Being

The World of Humanity represents the world of objective reality we see as *outside ourselves*. As a world of form, it provides the setting in which we live our everyday human lives, as well as the reality we experience through our five senses. It holds the energy patterns of death, change, fear, limitation, and duality. This world provides us with the environment in which we, as spiritual beings, can experience being human. This means having a physical body and working with (and possibly transcending) a particular energy pattern associated with the World of Humanity that we may have specifically 'come in' to work with.

The World of Divine Truth, on the other hand, has no physical form and already carries the energy pattern of eternal life, immutability, infinite abundance, love, and oneness with God. Even though we cannot perceive this world with our senses, and we scarcely possess the mental capacity to comprehend it, we can get enough of a sense of it to know that it is real. Such activities as prayer, meditation and Radical Forgiveness, all of which raise our vibration, allow us to access the World of Divine Truth.

These *existential realms* differ not in terms of place or time but solely in their vibrational level. The study of quantum physics has proven that all reality consists of energy patterns and that consciousness sustains these energy patterns. Thus, the world of form exists as dense concentrations of energy vibrating at frequencies we can experience through our physical senses. On the other hand, we experience the World of Divine Truth as an inner knowing and an extrasensory awareness.

48

Because these two worlds exist on the same continuum, we do not live sometimes in one and sometimes in the other. We live in both worlds at the same time. However, which world we experience at any given moment depends upon our awareness of them. Obviously, as human beings our consciousness resonates easily with the World of Humanity. Our senses naturally pull us into that world and convince us that it is real. Though some people are less grounded in the world of objective reality than others, human beings, on the whole, are firmly entrenched at this end of the continuum — which is how it should be.

Our awareness of the World of Divine Truth is limited, and this too appears to be by design. Our soul enters into this world to experience being human — thus our memory and awareness of the World of Divine Truth must be limited to allow us the full experience. We would not be able to take on fully the energies of change, fear, death, limitation, and duality that characterize this world if we knew they were illusory. If we incarnated with this memory, we would deny ourselves the opportunity to transcend these states and *to discover* that they are, indeed, simply illusions. By forgetting who we are when we take on a physical body, we give ourselves the chance to remember that we are spiritual beings having a physical experience.

During a gathering in Atlanta in 1990, I heard Gerald Jampolsky, a well known author and authority on *A Course In Miracles*, tell a true story about a couple returning home from the hospital after giving birth to their second child.

49

It is a story that illustrates the fact that we have a true knowing of our connection with God and our own soul but that we forget it fairly quickly after taking on a body. The couple was conscious of the need to include their three-year-old daughter in the celebration of the new baby's homecoming. But they felt perturbed by her insistence that she be allowed to go alone into the room with the baby. To honor her request, yet oversee the situation, they switched on the baby monitor so they could at least hear what was going on, if not see it. What they heard astounded them. The little girl went straight to the crib, looked through the bars at the newborn child, and said, "Baby, tell me about God. I'm beginning to forget."

The soul normally experiences no limitation. However, when it incarnates, the soul creates a personality, or Ego, that carries the particular characteristics it needs for its healing journey and chooses to forget its connection to the World of Divine Truth.

In spite of the veil we lower over the memory of our oneness with God, which the above story suggests might become fully drawn around the age of three, as humans we are not denied a connection to the World of Divine Truth. Our soul carries a vibration that resonates with the World of Divine Truth and connects us to that world.

We can aid this connection through practices like meditation, prayer, yoga, breathwork, dancing, and chanting. Through such practices we raise our vibration enough to resonate with that of the World of Divine Truth.

There is evidence to suggest that even this is changing rapidly. Everywhere I go I ask the same question of my workshop participants. *"How many of you are aware of a quickening or a speedup in our spiritual evolution — and that we are being asked by Spirit to move more quickly through our lessons in preparation for a profound shift of some kind?"* There is almost unanimous concurrence. More and more people now talk openly and freely about always being in touch with their 'guidance' and are willing to trust it more each day. The veil between the two worlds is definitely becoming thinner. Radical Forgiveness contributes to this process both at the individual level and at the level of collective awareness.

Yet the two types of forgiveness remain literally worlds apart. They each demand a different way of looking at the world and at life. Clearly, traditional forgiveness offers itself as *a way of living in the world* while Radical Forgiveness is nothing less than *a spiritual path.*

In terms of our capacity to heal ourselves and to evolve spiritually, Radical Forgiveness offers extraordinary potential to transform consciousness, and this potential far exceeds what is possible with traditional forgiveness.

Yet, we must recognize that we all still live in the World of Humanity, and at certain times we will fall short of what we might think of as the spiritual ideal. When we find ourselves immersed in pain, for example, it becomes virtually impossible for us to move into Radical Forgiveness. When we have recently experienced harm at the

51

hand of another, such as when we have just been raped, we cannot be expected to accept, in that moment, that the experience was something we wanted and that it represents the unfoldment of a Divine plan. We will not have the receptivity necessary to entertain that idea. It can only come later in moments of quiet reflection, not in the heat of anger and in the immediate aftermath of a trauma.

But then again, we must continually remind ourselves that what we have created IS the spiritual ideal; that we have created circumstances in our lives that help us grow and learn; that the lessons we need to learn are contained in the situation and that the only way to obtain the growth from the experience is to go *through* it.

The choice we have in this is not so much as to whether to have the experience (Spirit decides this for us), but how long we are going to hang out in victim consciousness because of it. Should we choose to quickly let go of the victim it is comforting to know that we have a technology that will make that happen. Traditional forgiveness by contrast has little to offer in this regard.

Summary:

- **Traditional Forgiveness** is firmly rooted in the World of Humanity. In the same way that the World of Humanity holds the energy of duality, so traditional forgiveness polarizes and judges everything as either good or bad, right or wrong. *Radical Forgiveness takes the view that there is no right/wrong or good/bad. Only our thinking makes it so.*

- **Traditional Forgiveness** always begins with the assumption that something wrong took place, and someone 'did something' to someone else. The victim archetype remains operative. *Radical Forgiveness begins with the belief that nothing wrong happened, and there are no victims in any situation.*

- **Traditional Forgiveness** is effective to the extent that it calls upon the highest human virtues, such as compassion, tolerance, kindness, mercy, and humility. These qualities point towards forgiveness and have healing potential. However, in and of themselves, they are not forgiveness. *Radical Forgiveness is no different in this regard since it also calls for these same virtues to be present in the process.*

- **Traditional Forgiveness** depends entirely upon our own capacity to feel compassion, so it is limited in this regard. No matter how much compassion or tolerance we muster for someone like Hitler, and no matter how much we empathize with the pain of his upbringing, nothing enables

53

us to forgive him (using traditional forgiveness) for the mass murder of six million Jews. *Radical Forgiveness has no limits whatsoever and is completely unconditional. If Radical Forgiveness cannot forgive Hitler, it can forgive nobody. Like unconditional love, it's all or nothing.*

• With **Traditional Forgiveness**, the Ego and our personality-self call the shots. Hence, the problem always appears 'out-there' with someone else. *With Radical Forgiveness, the finger points the other way — the problem lies 'in here,' with me.*

• **Traditional Forgiveness** believes in the reality of the physical world, in the complete integrity of 'what happens' and always tries to 'figure it all out' and thus, control the situation. *Radical Forgiveness recognizes the illusion, sees that what happened was just a story and responds by surrendering to the perfection of the situation.*

• **Traditional Forgiveness** does not factor in the notion of a spiritual mission and maintains its belief in, and fear of, death. *Radical Forgiveness sees death as an illusion and takes the view that life is eternal.*

• **Traditional Forgiveness** views life as a problem to be solved or punishment to be avoided. It experiences life as a random set of circumstances that just happen to us for no reason — thus, the origin of the popular bumper sticker, 'S__ happens!' *Radical Forgiveness sees life as entirely purposeful and motivated by love.*

54

- **Traditional Forgiveness** recognizes the inherent imperfection of human beings but fails to see the *perfection in the imperfection.* It cannot resolve that paradox. ***Radical Forgiveness exemplifies that paradox.***

- **Traditional Forgiveness** can carry a high vibration similar to Radical Forgiveness when calling upon some of the highest of human virtues, like kindness, humility, compassion, patience, and tolerance. The portal through which we begin the journey of raising our vibration to connect with the world of Divine Truth and experience **Radical Forgiveness** is the open heart.

- **Traditional Forgiveness,** when of a very high vibration, recognizes the profundity of the spiritual insight that we *all* are imperfect and that imperfection characterizes the nature of humanity. When we look at a wrongdoer through these eyes, we can say in all humility and with tolerance and compassion, "There, but for the Grace of God, go I." We own that we, too, are completely capable of whatever the accused person has done. If we are acquainted with our shadow-self, we know that we all have within us the potential to cause harm, to murder, to rape, to abuse children, and to annihilate six million people. This knowledge allows us to call forth our humility and makes us kind and merciful not only to the accused but to ourselves, for in them we recognize our own inherent imperfection, our own shadow. This recognition brings us very close to actually taking back that which we projected — the vital first step in Radical Forgiveness. ***Radical Forgiveness also lovingly sees***

55

TRADITIONAL FORGIVENESS	vs.	RADICAL FORGIVENESS
World of Humanity (Ego)	vs.	World of Divine Truth (Spirit)
Low vibratory rate	vs.	High vibratory rate
Something wrong happened	vs.	Nothing wrong happened
Judgment based	vs.	Judgment and blame free
Past orientation	vs.	Present time orientation
Need to figure it all out	vs.	Surrendering to what is as is
Victim consciousness	vs.	Grace consciousness
Judges human imperfection	vs.	Accepts human imperfection
What happened did (true)	vs.	Symbolic meaning of it (truth)
Physical reality only	vs.	Metaphysical realities
Problem is still 'out there'	vs.	Problem is with me (my error)
Letting go of resentment	vs.	Embracing the resentment
You and I are separate	vs.	You and I are ONE
'Shit happens'	vs.	There are no accidents
Life is random events	vs.	Life is purposeful
Personality (ego) in control	vs.	Soul following a divine plan
Reality is what happens	vs.	Reality is what we create
Death is real	vs.	Death is an illusion

For more explanation of these distinctions, see
Chapter 15: Articles of Faith.

Fig. 4: Distinctions between Traditional and Radical Forgiveness

the imperfection inherent in human beings but sees the perfection in the imperfection.

• **Radical Forgiveness** recognizes that forgiveness cannot be willed or bestowed. We must *be willing* to forgive and to give the situation over to our Higher Power. Forgiveness of any kind comes not from effort but from being open to experiencing it.

What is NOT Forgiveness:

While we are dealing with definitions, we should also be clear about what is NOT forgiveness. A lot of what passes for forgiveness is what I call *pseudo forgiveness*.

Lacking authenticity, pseudo forgiveness is usually just neatly packaged judgment and concealed resentment *masquerading* as forgiveness. The willingness to forgive is not there, and far from decreasing victim consciousness, actually expands it. However, the line between this and ordinary forgiveness may not be easy to determine.

Examples of Pseudo Forgiveness:

The following examples are listed in order of descending clarity, beginning with ones that are obviously false and ending with those that come close to traditional forgiveness.

• *Forgiving out of a sense of obligation* — This is totally inauthentic, yet many of us forgive from this place.

57

We think of forgiveness as the *right* thing or even the *spiritual* thing to do. We think we *ought* to forgive.

- *Forgiving out of a sense of righteousness* — This is the antithesis of forgiveness. If you forgive people because you think you are right and they are stupid, or because you pity them, that is pure arrogance.

- *Bestowing forgiveness or pardoning* — This is pure self-delusion. We do not possess the power to bestow forgiveness on anyone. When we bestow forgiveness, we *play God*. Forgiveness is not something we control — it just happens when we are willing.

- *Pretending Forgiveness* — pretending that we are not angry about something when we actually are angry provides not so much an opportunity to forgive but an opportunity to deny our anger. This represents a form of self- invalidation. When we do this we allow others to treat us like the proverbial doormat. Such behavior usually stems from a fear of not forgiving, of being abandoned, or from a belief that expressing anger is unacceptable.

- *Forgive and Forget* — This simply creates denial. Forgiveness is never simple erasure. Wise people forgive but *do not* forget. They strive to appreciate the gift inherent in the situation and to remember the lesson it taught them.

- *Making Excuses* — When we forgive, we often do it with explanations or by making excuses for the person we are forgiving. For example, we might say about our parents, "My father abused me, because he was abused by his own parents. He was doing the best he could." Forgiveness should be about letting go of the past and refusing to be controlled by it. If an explanation helps one to let go it might be helpful to that extent, though an explanation does not remove the idea that something wrong happened. Therefore, at best, it can only be traditional forgiveness. It also possesses a certain righteousness, which may mask anger. On the other hand, understanding why someone did what they did and having empathy for them connects us again to our own imperfection and opens the door to feeling compassion and mercy — leading to a higher vibration of traditional forgiveness but still falling short of Radical Forgiveness.

- *Forgiving the person but not condoning the behavior.* This largely intellectual approach may only masquerade as forgiveness, because it remains judgmental and self-righteous. It also has practical and semantic problems. How do you separate a murderer from the act of murder?

This last one raises the whole issue of accountability and responsibility which is the subject of the next chapter.

4: Accountability

I t needs to be clearly understood that Radical Forgiveness does not relieve us from responsibility in this world. We are spiritual beings having a human experience in a world governed by both physical and man-made laws, and as such, we are necessarily held to account for all our actions. That is an inherent part of the human experience which cannot be avoided.

In other words, when we create circumstances that hurt other people, we must accept that in the World of Humanity there are consequences for such actions. While, from a Radical Forgiveness standpoint, we would say that all parties involved in the situation are getting what they need, it is also true that experiencing the consequences — like going to jail, being fined, being shamed and condemned are all part of the lesson and are perfect once again in that spiritual context.

I am often asked whether, in a situation where someone has done us harm and where the normal reaction would be to seek redress through the courts, a forgiving person would actually take that course of action? The answer is, "*Yes*." We live in the World of Humanity which operates within the parameters of the Law of Cause

61

and Effect. This states that for every action there is a correspondingly equal reaction. Thus, early on we learn that our actions have consequences. If we were never held accountable for the harm we do, forgiveness would be meaningless and valueless. With no accountability put upon us, it would appear as if, no matter what we did, no one cared. Such action or attitude offers no compassion whatsoever. For instance, children always interpret *rightful* parental discipline applied appropriately as caring and loving. Conversely, they interpret being given total license by their parents as non-caring. Children know.

However, the extent to which we respond to other people's actions with a sense of righteous indignation, grievance, revenge, and resentment, rather than with a genuine desire to balance the scales with regard to principles of fairness, freedom and respect for others, determines our level of forgiveness. Righteousness and revenge lower our vibration. Conversely, defense of principles and acting with integrity raises our vibration. The higher the vibration, the closer we come to Divine Truth and the more able we are to forgive radically.

I recently heard bestselling author, Alan Cohen, tell a story that illustrates this point well. A friend of his once got involved in circumstances that resulted in a girl's death. For her wrongful death, he was imprisoned for many years. He accepted the responsibility for what had happened and behaved in every way as a model prisoner. However, the girl's father, a rich and influential man with friends in high places, made a vow to keep this man locked up for as many years as possible. So, every time this man became eligible for parole, the girl's father spent a great deal of time and money pulling every political string possible to make sure parole was denied. After numerous such occurrences, Cohen asked his friend how he felt about being denied parole because of this man's efforts to keep him in prison. The man said he forgave the girl's father every day of his life and prayed for him, because he realized that it was the father who was in prison, not himself.

In truth, the father who was unable to get beyond his rage, sadness and grief, was controlled by his need for revenge. He could not escape the prison of his own victimhood. Even traditional forgiveness was beyond him. Cohen's friend on the other hand, refused to be a victim and saw love as the only possibility. His vibration was higher and he was able to practice Radical Forgiveness.

Getting back to the issue of whether or not to seek redress through the courts, we should seek to make others accountable for their actions. Remember, though, that once we decide to sue, we must, as they say in AA, "pray for the S.O.B.," and for ourselves. (By the way, we do not have to like someone to forgive them!) In other words, we turn the matter over to our Higher Power. We recognize that Divine Love operates in every situation and that each person receives exactly what they want. We recognize that perfection always resides somewhere in the situation, even if it is not apparent at the time.

I had occasion to experience this myself when I had just completed this book and was looking around for someone to help me market it. A friend recommended someone so my wife, JoAnna, and I went to see her. She seemed OK and I had no reason to doubt her skill or integrity. However — it's funny how the Universe works — the deadline for getting the title into 'Books in Print,' was the next day. This is the reference book that bookstores use to order so it was important to get in then - or miss a whole year. But that also meant I was rushed into signing a contract with this woman. It also meant coming up with $4,000 which is what she wanted up-front as well as 15% of the book sales. We didn't have $4,000 but JoAnna somehow came up with $2,900. We would pay the rest in monthly installments. So we signed. Though rushed into it, I was pleased that I had delegated that part of the project.

Well, as the months went by, and well after my book was published, I noticed that I was still having to do a lot of what I thought I had contracted with her to do. I was booking all my own book signings, sending books to reviewers and so on. I wasn't seeing any results from her efforts at all. I kept my eye on it, but after a while I confronted her. It turned out that she had hardly done a thing. Of course she denied it and defended herself, but when I demanded to see letters and evidence of activity, there was nothing. I fired her, voided the contract for nonperformance and demanded my money back. Of course, she refused. So I started court proceedings to recoup the money.

As you can imagine, I was pretty upset. I was stuck where all people who imagine themselves victimized go— 'victimland!' And I was totally unconscious. I had my victim's story all made up and took every opportunity to share it with anyone who would listen. As far as I was concerned, she stole that money from me, and I needed to get even. I was well and truly stuck and I stayed that way for several weeks. And I was supposed to be *Mr. Forgiveness!*

Fortunately, a friend who had come to my first workshop many years ago came to dinner. When I told her my story, her response was, "Well, have you done a worksheet around this?" Of course, I hadn't. It was the thing furthest from my mind. "No, I haven't done a worksheet," I replied feeling very angry. "Don't you think you should?" Lucie asked. "No, I don't want to do an darn worksheet," I shouted.

Then JoAnna chimed in. "Well, it's your worksheet. You ought to practice what you preach!" That did it. Feeling cornered I stamped upstairs to get one but I was angry and I knew, and so did they, that I was doing it under protest. It was the last thing in the world I wanted to do, but they wouldn't let me off the hook. I still did each step in a huff and with little or no commitment to the process. Then all of a sudden, as I got about half way through, I had to read the statement — 'I release the need to blame and the need to be right.' That's when it hit me. *The need to be right!* All of a sudden it flashed before me what I was trying to be right about. I had a core belief that I always had to do everything myself! I saw that this incident was just another out-playing of that belief. All the other times I had unconsciously created being let down that way flashed before my eyes. I then saw and fully understood that this woman was supporting me in becoming acquainted with my toxic belief so I could release it and open myself to greater abundance.

Suddenly, all my anger evaporated and I saw how I had shut myself off from the very things I believed in and was teaching. I felt very ashamed. But at least I was conscious again. I could now see that this woman was an *'angel of healing'* for me, and I switched from feeling anger and resentment to feeling profound gratitude and love for her.

Besides having that wonderful healing, it was a very powerful and humbling lesson in how easy it is to go unconscious about spiritual law and how quickly your Ego will suck you into a drama and keep you there. It was a frightening demonstration of the power of my Ego to separate me from my Source and from everything I know to be true. It was also a powerful demonstration of why you need spiritual friends who will support you by not buying into your victim story and being prepared to challenge you on it.

However, the question you are probably asking is, having realized that she was a healing angel for me, did I cancel the court case against her? Well, I can tell you I agonized over this.

I recognized that, even though I now saw the truth from the perspective of the World of Divine Truth, the situation itself was deeply grounded in the World of Humanity. So I offered to mediate twice and she refused on both occasions.

I therefore went ahead with the court case reasoning that her soul needed to have that experience, otherwise it would have taken her out of it when I offered to mediate. But I went into it with my heart open and with the intention that the right and perfect outcome would ensue. The court found in my favor and I got a judgment against her for most of the $4,000. I never got the money, but that didn't matter. The point was that we had trusted the process and did what seemed to be necessary at the time.

And the truth is, it wouldn't have mattered which way I had decided. Spirit would have worked it out some other way and it all would have worked out OK in the end — as it always does. The idea that our decisions matter in the overall scheme of things is just our Ego trying to make us feel separate and special. The Universe has everything handled no matter what we decide. But how we make those decisions — whether from love or fear, greed or generosity, false pride or humility, dishonesty or integrity — matters to us personally because each decision we make affects our vibration.

Another situation I am often asked to address is when one becomes aware of a child being abused. The question raised is that if we assume that the child's spiritual growth is being supported by this experience, should we take action or not, since to interfere would be to deny the child's soul its growth experience? My answer is always that, as human beings, we must do what it is right according to our present awareness of right and wrong — as defined in human law. So we act accordingly while at the same time knowing that, in spiritual law, nothing wrong is taking place. Naturally then, we would

67

intervene. As human beings, we could not do otherwise. But our intervention is not wrong or right either, because either way, Spirit has it handled.

My reasoning is that if it were in the best interests of the child's soul for there to be no intervention, Spirit would arrange things in such a way as to prevent it. In other words, if I were not supposed to intervene, Spirit would keep me unaware of the situation. Conversely, if Spirit makes me aware of the situation, I assume it has no problem with me intervening. In the end, it is not even my decision.

When I do intervene however, I do it free of judgment and the need to blame anyone. I just do it, knowing that the Universe set the whole thing up for a reason and that there is a perfection in there somewhere.

5: Radical Forgiveness Therapy

There's little about Jill's story that is unusual. The reality is, it could be anyone's story. In fact, since the publication of the first edition of this book in 1997, many thousands of people have written, called or e-mailed me to say that they identify so much with it that they felt it was their own personal story. For many of those who have read it, this compelling story has been the beginning of their healing, just as it was for Jill.

Insofar as it is typical of many apparent relationship problems, this story also provides a good example of how Radical Forgiveness can be applied to the quite ordinary problems of every day life and demonstrates its viability as a radical alternative to traditional counseling and psychotherapy. It became known as Radical Forgiveness Therapy (RFT).

There is some irony in this since it is a principle of Radical Forgiveness that, notwithstanding all evidence to the contrary, nothing wrong is happening and that there is nothing to change. How can it therefore be therapy? After all, the main principle underlying Radical Forgiveness is that *without exception, everything that happens to us is Divinely guided, purposeful and for our greater good.*

But the very notion of therapy implies that something is amiss and needs to be changed. When we go to a therapist, we expect our therapist to ask himself or herself these three basic questions.

1. What is wrong with this person or circumstance?
2. What caused him/her to become this way?
3. How can his/her problem be fixed?

Since none of these questions are applicable to Radical Forgiveness how can Radical Forgiveness become a therapeutic modality? The answer lies in the way it worked for Jill.

You might recall that in the beginning of the story with Jill, I acted out of an implicit *agreement* with her that she really did have a problem, that Jeff was the basic cause of it and that the only way to react to it was by trying to find a solution. For quite some time I went down this traditional road with her. Only when I thought the time was right did I suggest a different (Radical Forgiveness), approach.

At that point I had to make it very clear to her that I was shifting the conversation in an entirely different direction and using an alternate set of assumptions. More particularly, I was shifting to a new set of questions. These were:

1. What is perfect about what is occurring for her?
2. How is this perfection being revealed?
3. How can she shift her viewpoint so she might become

willing to accept that there might be a certain perfection in her situation?

I can assure you that Jill's original perception of the situation with Jeff, and of all prior situations with her previous husband, certainly did not jive with the idea of everything being perfect. Indeed, she felt that what had occurred was *self-evidently* wrong or bad. Most people would have agreed with her.

However, as we saw, the healing occurred for her only when she realized that, in fact, there was no right or wrong in any of the situations and that she was clearly not being victimized by anyone and that far from being her enemy, Jeff was her healing angel. She slowly began to see how at every moment Divine guidance was helping her heal an earlier misperception and related false belief system that for years had prevented her from expressing her true self. Each situation, including what was happening with Jeff, was on that basis, a gift of grace.

This actually makes RFT less of a therapy and more of a process of education. The therapist or coach as I prefer to call him or her, acts not so much out of a desire to fix someone as to enlighten him or her. Radical Forgiveness is a spiritual philosophy that has practical application to peoples' lives insofar as it gives them a spiritual perspective that they can use to apply, in the manner of self-help, to whatever problem or situation that they are dealing with.

The Divine plan is not something fixed. At any point in the unfoldment of one's plan, one is always at choice. Radical Forgiveness helps people shift their viewpoint and make new choices based on their insights.

Jill's story demonstrates how difficult making that shift in perception can be. Even with fairly obvious clues, it took a lot of discussion and a lot of processing of emotional pain before Jill became open to understanding a different interpretation. This especially was true of her former husband's supposed infidelity.

Imagine how tough it might be to sell the idea of Radical Forgiveness to a holocaust victim or to someone who has just been raped or otherwise violently abused. Indeed, much of RFT's preliminary work involves creating a willingness to even look at the *possibility* of there being perfection in what happened. Even then, depending on the circumstances, developing such a receptivity can take time and almost always requires a great deal of emotional release work first. It is nevertheless possible. I can say that because I have seen people with horrendous stories make tremendous shifts in very short periods of time.

Yet, it remains possible that some people may never get to the point where they become receptive. They simply may never get beyond their feelings of victimhood. On the other hand, those who do find themselves able to see, even for a moment, the perfection in their situation, are empowered to release their feelings of victimhood and to become free.

Jill was one of those. She and Jeff remain together and happily married to this day.

Therein lies the power of this work, for, as we shall see in later chapters, releasing victimhood provides the key to health, personal power and spiritual evolution. We have been addicted to the victim archetype for eons, and as we move into the Aquarian Age (the next 2,000 year period of spiritual evolution), we must answer the call to let go of the past, release the victim archetype and be more aware of life occurring in the moment.

There are some prerequisites, however, to doing so. First, the receptivity that Radical Forgiveness ultimately depends upon requires our being open to seeing things from a spiritual standpoint. It references no particular religion and excludes none, but it does require at least a belief in a Higher Power or Higher Intelligence and the idea of a spiritual reality beyond our own physical world. A strictly atheistic viewpoint would not allow Radical Forgiveness to occur, nor RFT to work. We shall see that to make Radical Forgiveness a reality in our lives, we need to be comfortable with the idea that we can walk in both worlds simultaneously.

Having said that, Radical Forgiveness can be explained in non-threatening terms and in such language as to honor all people's religious beliefs. It can be explained in ways that provide a fit with their existing belief systems, thus allowing them to listen with comfort. Besides that, a substantial part of Radical Forgiveness Therapy (RFT), does not depend upon mystical or esoteric ideas for its validity. Repression, denial and projection all are concepts firmly rooted in psychological theory. Therefore, these mechanisms can be explained fully in scientific terms.

I cannot stress enough that mixing the traditional therapy with RFT will not work. The questions and the assumptions underlying the two forms are just too different. Any therapist who adds RFT to his or her tool kit must first of all be aware of the distinctions between RFT and traditional therapy and be able to clearly differentiate them to a client and second, must work hard to keep them separated.

In the main, Radical Forgiveness Therapy will be for people who are not in the least mentally sick — just needing some help dealing with the issues of daily life. However, if a person has profound issues and deeply repressed pain with complex defense mechanisms in place, that person should be referred to a qualified psychotherapist who also uses RFT.

The technology of Radical Forgiveness is deceptively simple and yet amazingly effective as therapy for the soul, — for individuals, groups, races and even countries. For example, I have held workshops for Jews and other persecuted people who hold the pain of their race or group and have witnessed amazing shifts in their consciousness. They have been able to let go of the collective pain and in so doing, I believe, help heal the collective consciousness of that group many generations back. I am currently applying this modality to helping heal the 200 year old story that began when the first English convicts arrived in Australia and began the systematic decimation of the aboriginal people. There is a great desire within the white population in Australia at this time to say "Sorry," and for the aboriginal people to forgive so that both may move on and become one Australia. In my book, *Reconciliation Through Radical Forgiveness,* published only in Australia, I argue that only a spiritual technology like Radical Forgiveness can bring reconciliation about and I have given them the tools to make it a reality. Then I will take it to other places in the world where there are racial divisions, including the U.S., and do the same thing.

Training and certification in Radical Forgiveness Coaching and Therapy is available through the **Institute for Radical Forgiveness Therapy and Coaching, Inc.,** based in Atlanta, Georgia. This is both for licensed professionals who wish to become certified Radical Forgiveness Practitioners, and for non-professionals who might simply wish to coach others in how to apply Radical Forgiveness to ordinary life-problems. Even in business, Radical Forgiveness is a valid concept and an extremely powerful technology for tracking where energy is stuck within the corporation or institution and for releasing it. The effect on profitability can be dramatic which is the reason why quite a number of business consultants have already taken the training. *(For further details see Appendix II, Page 297).*

6: The Mechanisms of the Ego

In matters of a spiritual nature, it is seldom long before the conversation turns to the Ego. Radical Forgiveness is no exception since the Ego does seem to play a central role. So, what constitutes the Ego and what role does it play in Radical Forgiveness?

I feel that there are at least two ways of answering this question. The first casts the Ego as our enemy, while the second sees it as our friend.

The *Ego-As-Enemy* viewpoint makes the Ego responsible for keeping us separated from Source out of self interest for its own survival. Consequently it is our spiritual enemy and we are at war with it. Many spiritual disciplines take this as their central idea and demand that the Ego must be dropped or transcended as a prerequisite for spiritual growth.

The *Ego-As-Friend* model sees the Ego as being the part of our own soul — a part that acts as our loving guide for this human experience.

I prefer to think that there is truth in both of these ideas even though at first blush they seem to be incompatible.

Let me explain each in turn, as I have come to understand them for myself, so you can make up your own mind.

1. Ego As The Enemy:

In this model the Ego is said to exist as a deeply-held set of beliefs about who we are in relationship to Spirit, formed when we experimented with the thought of separation from the Divine Source. In fact, we could say that the Ego is the belief that separation actually occurred.

At the moment of separation, so the story goes, the Ego had us believe that God had become very angry about our experiment. This immediately created enormous guilt within us. The Ego then elaborated on its story by telling us that God would get even and punish us severely for our great sin. So great was the guilt and the terror created in us by the belief that this story was true, we had no choice but to repress these emotions deep in our unconscious mind. This spared us from the conscious awareness of them.

This tactic worked quite well, yet we retained a great fear that the feelings might rise once again. To remedy this problem, the Ego developed a new belief — that the guilt lay with someone else rather than within ourselves. In other words, we began projecting our guilt on to other people so we could be rid of it entirely. They became our *scapegoats*. Then, to ensure that the guilt stayed with them, we became angry with them and kept up a continuous attack on them. *(For more detailed information on denial and projection, see Chapter Seven).*

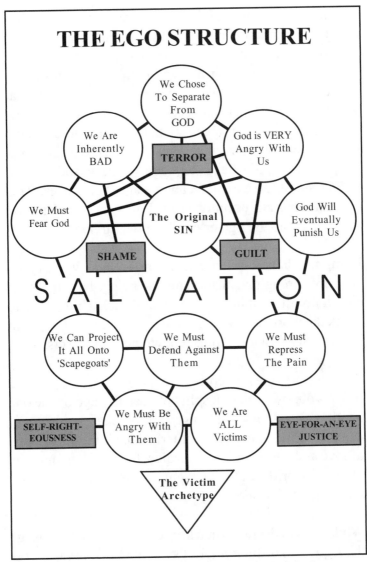

Fig. 5: The Structure of the Ego *(perspective #1)*

79

Herein lies the origin of the victim archetype and the human race's continual need to attack and to defend against each other. After attacking the people onto whom we projected our guilt, we fear them attacking us in return. So, we create strong defenses to protect ourselves and what we see as our complete innocence. At some level we know we are guilty, so the more we defend against the attack the more we reinforce our guilt. Thus, we must constantly find people to hate, to criticize, to judge, to attack, and to make wrong simply so we can feel better about ourselves. This dynamic constantly reinforces the Ego's belief system, and in this manner, the Ego ensures its own survival.

Using this behavior pattern as a reference, we can now see why, throughout history, human beings have had such a high investment in their anger and such a high need to break the world into victims and persecutors, villains and heroes, victors and vanquished, winners and losers.

Furthermore, the perception we have of a *we/they* world reflects our own internal split between the Ego on the one hand, which is the belief in separation, fear, punishment and death; and Spirit on the other, which is the knowledge of love and eternal life. We project this division onto the physical world by always seeing the enemy as *out there,* rather than within ourselves.

While all belief systems quickly become resistant to change the Ego is no ordinary belief system in this regard. It is extremely resistant to change. It holds incredible power in our unconscious mind and carries an enormous block of votes when it comes to making decisions about who we think we are. This belief system is so powerful that it appears to be an entity in its own right — and we have named it the Ego.

We have become trapped in the belief of separation to such a degree that it has become our reality. We have been living the myth of separation for eons, making real the idea that we chose separation by naming it the original sin.

In actuality, no separation ever occurred. We are as much a part of God as we always were. We are spiritual beings having a human experience, remember? Consequently there is no such thing as original sin in this sense.

Jesus purportedly gave us this revelation — the truth about our illusion — in *A Course In Miracles*, a three-volume work by Jesus channeled through a lady named Helen Schucman, the purpose of which was to show us the error of the Ego's way and to teach us that the way home to God is through forgiveness. *(Interestingly, Helen was a very reluctant channel and never did believe a word of what she channeled.)* Contrary to some prevailing Christian theology, many biblical scholars find these very same ideas expressed in the Bible.

Anyway, contrary to what the Ego would have us believe, the truth is that we actually come to the physical plane with God's blessing and His unconditional love. God always will honor our free will and our choices at the highest level and will offer no Divine intervention — unless asked.

81

Fortunately, Radical Forgiveness provides the perfect tool for asking for such assistance, because in the process, you demonstrate to God that you have seen beyond the Ego and glimpsed the truth — that only love is real — and that we are all One with God including those who seemed at first to be our enemy.

2. The Ego As Loving Guide:

This other, more friendly way of looking at the Ego — which I find equally tenable — holds that far from being our enemy, the Ego is a part of our soul; a part that splits off to play a guidance role in the World of Humanity in absolutely perfect and purposeful opposition to the Higher Self.

That role is to provide the anchor in the World of Humanity that would fully test our ability to be a spiritual being having a truly human experience. The only value in having the human experience is precisely to experience such things as the Ego provides: belief in duality, separateness and fear. Furthermore, that we need to experience them fully at the feeling level in order for us to wake up and remember that the opposites are true.

Our Ego then, in this model, is the guide that will take us on all these journeys into the illusion and try to teach us many false lessons that will keep us stuck in the illusion. But it does so, not out of malice nor even for the sake of its own survival, but because it loves us and knows that we need this experience for our spiritual growth.

82

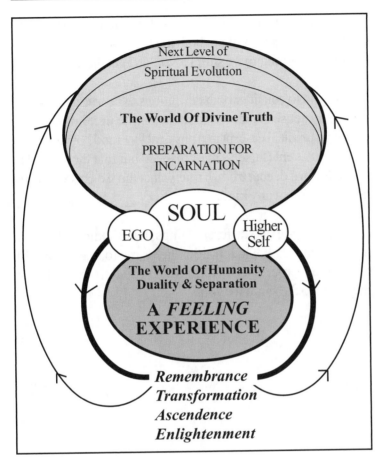

Fig. 6. The Soul's Journey

But the Ego does not do this alone. The Higher Self is our other guide who waits patiently while we journey into the illusion with the Ego until we are ready to hear the truth. It is through the gentle whispers of the Higher Self that we wake up, bit by bit, until we finally remember who we are and go home. That's what transformation is, and enlightenment too.

83

This is our Soul's journey while in physical form. And there exists no short cut. Without both the Ego and the Higher Self working their magic, we simply wouldn't get there.

I invite you to consider both definitions to be true at the same time. My sense is that the first one is true in terms of it explaining our initial descent into physical form and how we came to see that event (falsely) in retrospect, but that the second is grounded in a deeper truth, namely, that there exists within us no separation of any kind.

Maybe they are two different things, I don't know. It really doesn't matter. Each definition helps me to make sense of this human experience in terms of spiritual truth and I trust they will do the same for you.

7: Hideouts and Scapegoats

Understanding the role that the twin psychological ego-defense mechanisms of repression and projection play in how we heal relationships is essential to the concept of Radical Forgiveness. A closer inspection of the mechanisms of each might therefore be helpful.

Operating together, repression and projection wreak havoc upon our relationships and our lives. Together they create and maintain the victim archetype. Understanding how they work enables us to counteract the Ego's use of them to keep us separated from each other and from God.

1. Repression

Operating as a normal psychological defense mechanism, repression occurs when feelings like terror, guilt or rage become so overwhelming that the mind simply blocks them from conscious awareness entirely. This makes repression a powerful mental safety device, for without this blocking mechanism we easily could go mad. It works so effectively that absolutely no memory of the feelings, or the event which precipitated them remain — totally blocked out of conscious awareness for days, weeks or years — sometimes even for the rest of the lifetime.

Suppression:

Repression should not be confused with this other, similar but less severe, defense mechanism. Suppression occurs when we *consciously* refuse to acknowledge emotions that we do not want to feel or express. Though we know they are there, we try to push, or *stuff* them away and refuse to deal with them. However, continued denial of them for long periods of time may lead to a *numbness* equivalent to them becoming repressed.

Repressed Guilt and Shame

Guilt is a universal human experience. Deep in our unconscious mind we have such overwhelming guilt and shame about the thought, albeit not true, that we separated from God (the original sin), that we have no choice but to repress this feeling. We absolutely could not handle these emotions otherwise.

Please note that guilt and shame are not the same. We feel guilt when we feel we have *done* wrong. Shame takes us to a deeper level of guilt where we have a sense of actually *being* wrong. With shame, the Ego makes us feel inherently wrong at the very core of our being. No shame or guilt is as deep seated as the shame of the original sin, the central, but entirely false, plank of the Ego's belief system.

Shame Blocks Energy

Young children can be easily shamed, say, when they wet themselves, get an erection, show anger, act shy, and so on. While these may be natural occurrences, the children nevertheless feel the shame, and the cumulative effects of this feeling can become overwhelming. Consequently, they repress their shame, but it remains in the unconscious mind as well as in the body. It becomes locked into their system at the cellular level and becomes an energy block in the body. If left unresolved for too long, this block gives rise to either mental/emotional problems or physical problems or both. Repressed emotion now is recognized by many researchers to be one of the principal causes of cancer.

Repressed Feelings

A large trauma, such as the death of a parent, can cause a child to repress emotion. Likewise, something seemingly insignificant, such as a casual critical remark interpreted as meaningful, or an event incorrectly assumed to be his/her fault, can cause emotions to be repressed. For example, children nearly always interpret a divorce as their fault. Research suggests that children remember conversations their parents had while they were still in the womb. A discussion about an unwanted pregnancy before birth can lead to a child's feelings of being unwanted and fear of being abandoned. Such feelings would be repressed even at such an early time in the child's life.

Generational Guilt

Groups and even nationalities commonly repress accumulated generational guilt. Without doubt, this is the case now with black and white Americans over slavery. The racial problems we now experience in America all stem from the unresolved and repressed guilt within white people and un-resolved and repressed rage in the blacks.

The Dark Side

We also experience intense shame over aspects of our-selves that we dislike and, therefore, disown. Carl Jung, the famous Swiss psychiatrist, referred to this as our *shadow*, because it represents the dark side of ourselves, the part that we do not want to see or to have seen. This part of ourselves could kill another human being, knows we could have taken part in the killing of six million Jews had we been German during that time, knows we might have owned and brutalized slaves had we been born white in the South before the Civil War, could hurt or rape some-one, is greedy or avaricious, is rageful and vengeful, or is in some other way deviant or unacceptable. Any such char-acteristic of ourselves, or area of our lives that brings us feelings of shame, we classify as our shadow and then re-press it.

Sitting On a Volcano

Repressing this kind of energy is like sitting on a volcano! We never know when our strength will give out, thus al-lowing the lava (shadow) to spurt forth and wreak havoc on our world. This explains why we need to bring in a scapegoat on whom we can project all that shame. That way we can be free of it, at least temporarily.

88

2. Projection

Even when we have repressed the feelings and/or memories associated with a life event, we know, on an unconscious level, that the shame, guilt or self-criticism associated with it remains with us. So, we attempt to rid ourselves of that pain by *taking it out* of ourselves and transferring it on to someone, or something, else *outside* of ourselves. This projection process allows us to forget we ever possessed such feelings.

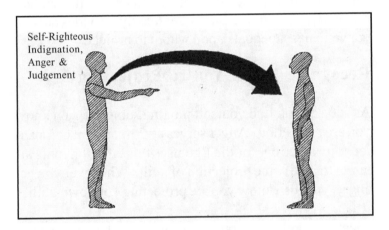

Self-Righteous Indignation, Anger & Judgement

Fig. 7: Projecting Our Repressed Shame

Once we project what we do not want to own onto someone else, we see them, rather than us, possessing those qualities. So, if we repress our guilt and then project it, we make that person the wrong one. If we repress our anger and then project it, we see them as the angry one. We can accuse them of all the things we feared we would be accused of ourselves. No wonder we feel so relieved when we project! In so doing, we make someone else responsible for everything terrible that happens to us or for what we see as negative about ourselves. Then, we can demand that they be punished, so we can feel even more righteous and safe from attack.

This explains why we love to watch the news on television. The news provides us with an opportunity to project all our guilt and shame on the murderers, rapists, corrupt politicians, and other *bad* people we see on the screen. After doing so, we can go to bed feeling okay about ourselves. The news, and all the other television programs that feature *bad* people and situations, endlessly provides us with convenient scapegoats upon whom to project.

Recognize When You're Projecting

As soon as you find yourself judging someone, you know you are projecting. Anger serves as the constant companion of projection, for the Ego uses this emotion in its attempt to justify the projection of guilt. Whenever you get angry, you also know you are projecting your own guilt.

What you find so objectionable about another person simply serves as a reflection of that part of you that you have rejected and denied in yourself (your shadow) and projected onto them instead. If this was not so, you would not be upset.

This concept — *what we attack and judge in others is really what we condemn in ourselves* — is the central idea behind Radical Forgiveness and the key to our own soul-level healing.

Resonance

We feel victimized by other people precisely because they resonate with our own guilt, anger, fear, or rage. (See next chapter.) It feels like they are *doing something to us* to make us angry. When we own that the feelings begin with us, not with them, we can drop the need to feel victimized.

The Attack/Defense Cycle

Though repression and projection are meant as temporary relief valves for the psyche, the Ego co-opted them as the means to maintain itself. Remember, the Ego simply consists of a set of beliefs, the central one being that we are separate from God. Following from that belief comes the belief that God is after us and when he catches us he will punish us severely. The Ego uses the dynamics of repression and projection to hide these beliefs, as well as the guilt and fear that accompanies them, from our consciousness. Hence, repression and projection become a permanent way of being for us. Our whole life revolves around our continual repression, denial and projection, all of which are maintained in perpetuity by the never-ending fear/attack and defense/attack cycles. This provides a perfect recipe for continual internal conflict.

The Drive For Wholeness

Fortunately, in spite of the incredible efficiency of repression and projection, the innate drive for wholeness emanating from our souls possesses more power than the Ego. This drive for wholeness originates from that part of us

91

that knows the truth and is not content to deny it and project it. This part, the soul, which cries out for a return to love, carries the same energy that creates our opportunities for learning and for healing — the energy of Radical Forgiveness.

Fear Of Intimacy

Every person we meet offers us the opportunity to choose between projection or forgiveness, union or separation. However, the more intimate we become with someone and the closer they get to our true self, the more likely it becomes that they will learn the guilty truth about us. This possibility of being *discovered* creates enormous fear inside us — and the temptation to project becomes almost irresistible. At this point, the honeymoon is over. The fear of intimacy becomes so strong that the relationship is likely to fall apart. Most do.

All Relationships Are For Healing

To move forward and succeed, we must understand this phenomenon and use Radical Forgiveness to stay in the relationship and to fulfill its true spiritual purpose — which is to heal the people involved.

As we saw in Jill's Story, Radical Forgiveness can certainly save marriages! However, this is not necessarily the goal. If the purpose of the relationship has been fulfilled, which is to say that the people are healed, the relationship may need to dissolve naturally and peacefully.

8: Attraction & Resonance

As we saw in the previous chapter, we project our guilt and anger onto people who have the capacity to *resonate* with our feelings, and such people become convenient scapegoats.

Just as a radio station uses a certain frequency to broadcast its programs, so our emotions (energy in motion) vibrate at certain frequencies. People who resonate with our feelings vibrate at that same rate and are likely to have a similar emotion pattern to our own - either the same or opposite - which they then mirror back to us.

Our core beliefs also have a certain frequency. By speaking them aloud, we give our beliefs even more energy, and they take on a causal quality in the Universe. Thus, our spoken beliefs cause effects in our world. In addition, other people *resonate* with the energetic frequency of that belief. In other words, they vibrate sympathetically at the same rate with it. When they do so, they are attracted into our lives to mirror our beliefs back to us. That gives us a chance to look at, and if necessary, to change our minds about that belief. It is not only negative beliefs that get mirrored back to us, either. For example, if we are loving and trusting, we will tend to attract people into our lives who are likewise trustworthy and nurturing.

Recall from Part 1 that my sister, Jill, had a belief that she would never be enough for any man. This belief resonated with a man who was a sexual addict. He provided the ideal partner for her, because he supported her belief by continually having sex with other women, thus showing her she was *not enough* for him. She did not make the connection in that relationship and, consequently, did not heal the pain that created this belief in the first place. So, she found another man (Jeff) who resonated with her belief. He supported her belief differently by using his own issue of co-dependence with his daughter, Lorraine, as the catalyst. In this situation, she saw the connection and realized that he was mirroring her belief that she was not enough, and both of them healed.

If you want to know what you dislike about yourself and have likely disowned, simply look at what annoys you about the people who come into your life. Look into the mirror they provide. If you seem to attract a lot of angry people into your life, you probably have not dealt with some anger of your own. If people seem to withhold love from you, some part of you is unwilling to give love. If people seem to steal things from you, part of you behaves dishonestly or feels dishonest. If people betray you, maybe you have betrayed someone in the past.

Look at the issues that upset you, too. If abortion really makes you mad maybe a part of you shows little reverence for life in other ways, or a part of you knows it could abuse a child. If you are passionately against homosexuality, maybe you cannot accept the part of you that sometimes feels homosexually inclined.

Hall of Mirrors

The reflection does not always appear that readily or as simply. For example, sometimes we do not identify with the specific behavior as much as we do with the underlying meaning it holds for us. A man who gets angry about his wife's overeating and obesity may not be resonating with any personal tendency to overeat; instead, he might be resonating with her use of food to avoid dealing with emotional problems, because it mirrors his tendency to run away from his own emotional problems. Clearly, seeing what others mirror for us can become like looking at the myriad of distorted images in a hall of mirrors.

Automatic Reversal of Projection

The beauty of Radical Forgiveness lies in the fact that it does not require that we recognize what we project. We simply forgive the person for what is happening at the time. In doing so, we automatically undo the projection no matter how complicated the situation. The reason for this is simple in that the person represents the original pain that caused us to project in the first place. As we forgive him/ her we clear that original pain. Moreover, no matter what we see as our problems, only one basic problem actually exists for any of us — our guilt about separating from God. All other problems derive from this original one.

Ironically, the people who seem to upset us the most are those who, at the soul level, love and support us the most. Almost always, and often at great expense to themselves in terms of their own discomfort, these individuals try to teach us something about ourselves and to encourage us to move towards healing. Remember, this is not a personality-to-personality exchange. In fact, more than likely the personalities of these individuals clash terribly. Instead, the souls of each player set up the scenario in the hope that the person will eventually see their issue and heal.

Don't Take Life So Personally

Who comes into our lives to help us accomplish this task is actually irrelevant. If one particular person does not take the job, somebody else will. The tragedy is that, as the victim, we seldom understand this. We imagine that we just happened to be the unlucky recipient of a particular person's harmful behavior. It does not occur to us that we might have (at the soul level) attracted the person and the situation to ourselves for a reason, and that had it not been this person, it simply would have been someone else. We mistakenly feel that but for this person we would not have had the problem. In other words, we see the problem as entirely with the other person, whom we now feel justified in hating and resenting for *causing* us pain and unhappiness.

Blaming Our Parents

We often hear this type of blame when people talk about their parents. "If I'd had different parents, I'd be whole and complete today," people say. Wrong. They could have chosen a different set of parents, that's true; but the new set would have given them the exact same experience, because that's what their soul wanted.

Repeating Relationship Patterns

When we see ourselves as victims, we think only about killing the messenger. We miss the message. This explains why people today go from marriage to marriage recreating the same relationship dynamic each time. They do not get the message with the first spouse, so they go on to another who continues trying to relay the message the last spouse tried to relay.

Co-dependency And Mutual Projection

We also find others onto whom we project our own self-hatred who will not only accept it but reciprocate by projecting theirs back onto us. We call this kind of agreement a co-dependent or addictive relationship. That special someone compensates for what we feel is missing in ourselves by continually telling us we are okay, so we avoid feeling our shame about who we are. We do the same thing for them in return, thus both people learn to manipulate each other with highly conditional love based on the underlying guilt. (The stereotypical Jewish Mother is a wonderful example of this archetype.) The moment the other person withdraws approval, we are forced to confront our guilt and self-hatred again, and everything collapses. Love turns immediately into hate, and each partner attacks the other. This explains why we see so many faltering relationships, that once seemed supportive and loving, turn into a cauldron of hate almost instantaneously.

97

9: Cause & Effect

Central to the idea that we create our own reality is the Law of Cause and Effect. This states that every action has an equal reaction. Therefore, every cause must have an effect, and every effect must have a cause. Since thoughts are causal in nature, every thought has an effect in the world. In other words, we — unconsciously for the most part — create our world, the world of humanity, with our thoughts.

When we vibrate at a high frequency, such as when we pray, meditate or contemplate, we can create consciously and intentionally through thought. Most of the time, however, we do so quite unconsciously. Individual random thoughts do not carry a lot of energy, so they create a relatively small effect. However, thoughts accompanied by larger amounts of energy, especially emotional or creative energy, have a much larger effect in the world. Thus, they play a larger hand in creating our reality.

When a thought gathers sufficient energy to become a belief, it has an even greater effect in the world. It becomes an operating principle in our lives, and we then create effects — circumstances, situations, even physical events that hold true to that belief. What we believe about the world is how it always will be for us.

Acceptance of the principle that thought is creative is fundamental to an understanding of Radical Forgiveness, for it allows us to see that what turns up in our lives represents what we have created with our thoughts and our beliefs. It allows us to see that we simply are projecting all our thoughts and beliefs about *the way things are* onto the world.

Projecting the Illusion

Metaphorically, we run a movie, called ***Reality***, through our mind (the projector), and we project it *out there*.

Fig. 8: Projecting Our Own Reality

Once we understand that what we call reality is just our projections, instead of blaming others we can begin to take responsibility for what we have created with our thoughts. When we change our perception and drop our attachment to our belief that what appears on the screen represents reality, we experience Radical Forgiveness.

100

Consciousness Determines What Happens

While it may seem difficult to see the principle of cause and effect operating in our lives, it becomes apparent when we trace back from what is occurring. In other words, if you want to know your beliefs, just look at what is happening. That will tell you what you are projecting. For example, if you keep getting attacked or disasters keep happening to you, the likelihood is that you believe the world is inherently an unsafe place. You are creating these events to prove that you are right about that and people are supporting you in this belief by appearing to you to behave in a threatening or dangerous manner.

Some friends of mine have a spiritual conference center in the mountains of North Carolina. Werner, being of a prudent nature, thought he and his wife, Jean, should have insurance to protect their buildings against fire, storm damage and the frequent tornadoes that come through each season. Jean was very much against the idea. She felt having such insurance would clearly indicate to the Universe that they did not trust in their safety. Now, I am not advocating this, but they decided against purchasing the insurance.

The following year, a huge storm hit their very mountain and devastated the area. Thousands of trees were uprooted and thrown down. When my wife and I drove up to visit them two weeks later, we couldn't believe our eyes. It looked like a war zone. They had obviously been obliged to cut their way out. The storm had happened while 36 people were at the center attending a conference, and they were unable to leave for two whole days. However, in spite of all the trees down, not one car nor any of the buildings were touched — and both were right in amongst the trees. Trees fell within inches of structures and autos but miraculously damaged nothing. For my friends, it was a great confirmation of their faith and willingness to trust.

Looking at this from a cause and effect standpoint, Jean recognized that buying insurance reinforced a belief (a cause) in adversity and would create the energy for something bad (an effect) to happen. Instead she chose the thought (cause) "We are doing God's work here, and we are totally safe." The effect, as it played out in the world, was that in the midst of chaos nothing bad happened.

As I have said, if you want to know your beliefs, look at what you have in your life — or what you do not have in your life. If, for example, you do not have love in your life and do not seem to be able to create a loving relationship, examine your beliefs about self-worthiness, or about safety with the opposite sex. Of course, this may not be as easy as it sounds, for the beliefs you hold may be buried deep in your subconscious mind.

You Don't Need To Know Why

The good news is that you do not have to know why you created your situation or what beliefs led you to its creation. Just seeing the situation's existence as an opportunity to perceive it differently — *being willing* to see it as perfect — is enough to bring about the required shift in perception and a healing of the original pain.

The truth is, from the World of Humanity we cannot know *why* a situation is as it is, because the answer lies in the world of Divine Truth; and we can know little to nothing of that world as long as we are in human form. *All we can do is surrender to the situation.*

Just Surrender

If new insights, connections, old memories, emotional movements, and other psychic events are necessary for the desired change to occur, they will happen automatically and without our conscious control. If we try to figure it all out and manipulate the unfolding process, this creates resistance and blocks the process completely, which puts us right back under the influence of the Ego.

Freedom From the Law

It is therefore important to realize that the Law of Cause and Effect only applies to the World of Humanity. It is a physical law, not a spiritual law. Creating a parking space or any other physical thing that you desire and create with your mind is still only manipulating the illusion. It has little to do with being spiritual as such. In fact, if we imagine that we are special because of how well we can manifest in the world, this simply increases our sense of separation and strengthens the Ego.

On the other hand, when we truly drop the need to know the why or how of everything, let go of our need to control the world and truly surrender to what is — as is, in the knowledge that the love of God is in everything, we shall transcend the Law of Cause and Effect entirely. Then we shall realize that karma is just another story that exists only in our minds in the World of Humanity. In the World of Divine Truth, there is no such thing as Karma or Cause and Effect. There is only first cause which is God.

However, if we engage in activities and consistent ways of being that result in our vibration being significantly raised *(through the continual and sustained use of Radical Forgiveness over a long period of time for instance)*, we may find ourselves becoming 'first cause.'

That would be in stark contrast to how it is for the majority of us at the present time, where we are always the 'effect' in this cause-and-effect world — always having to react to what appears to be happening 'out there.'

Perhaps, in the not-too-distant future, when our vibratory rate is raised and we have all our energy and consciousness in present time rather than tied up in past or future, we will find ourselves not so much 'noticing' sychronicities as 'becoming' synchronicity itself.

For more on how to gauge your own vibratory rate, how you stack up against the 'enlightened' ones and how many it would take of a certain vibration to shift planetary consciousness, I recommend David Hawkins's book, "Power vs. Force," published by Hay House.

10: Mission "Forgiveness"

Not one of us can feel our soul's journey to be over until we (as an entire species) have completed the mission we created for ourselves. This is no less than to transform the energies of fear, death and duality by coming to the full realization that we are not separated from God at all and that these energies are simply illusion. This is our collective mission. Each of us serves as an individual expression of that mission, and the life we create for ourselves here in the World of Humanity purely serves that purpose. There are no exceptions. Whether we know it or not, we are all on that spiritual path.

Our Individual Mission

The decision about which energies we work with is not decided by us at the human level. That decision predates our incarnation and is made by our soul group — a group to which we belong made up of souls who either incarnate with us or act as our spirit guides during our incarnation.

Once it is decided which energies we shall work with, we then carefully choose parents who will provide the experiences we need as children and arrange for others to come along at the right time to play their respective roles in the experiences necessary to the accomplishment of our mission. We then create dramas throughout our physical lives that allow us to experience the feelings or energies that make up our mission. These dramas serve as opportunities for us to see the illusion, forgive, heal, and, in so doing, remember who we are.

Mission Amnesia

Seen from the World of Divine Truth prior to incarnation, the mission seems easy. However, once we incarnate it takes on a new level of difficulty. This is due not only to the greater density of energy in the World of Humanity but because the mission must be undertaken free of any awareness that we have chosen this experience. If we knew (remembered) the truth about our purpose, the experience would be senseless. How can we remember who we are if we have never forgotten? So, Spirit creates the human experience in such a way that when we are born into our bodies we lose all recall of our mission and all awareness that life on the physical plane is, in fact, *a setup*.

To accomplish our mission (to transform energies) we must have a total experience of those energies. For example, to transform the energy of *victim*, we must feel totally victimized. To transform the energy of fear, we must feel terrorized. To transform the energy of hate, we must be consumed with hatred. In other words, we must go fully into the experience of being human. It is only when we have fully felt the emotions connected with these energies that we gain the ability to move into the full forgiveness of them. And, it is in forgiving them that we remember who we are.

From this viewpoint, clearly we are never in a position to judge anyone. A person who appears hateful may have chosen to transform that energy as his mission. Thus, his hateful behavior, even though it seems to harm others *(who may have volunteered to have hate projected at them as their mission)*, is neither right nor wrong. His hateful behavior simply represents what needs to happen to transform the energy of hate. Period.

The energy of hate is transformed when someone who feels hated sees the love beneath the hate and forgives the person for hating him. In that moment, hearts open and love flows between the two people. Thus, hate is transformed into love.

Janet's Story

Janet, who had cancer, attended one of my early cancer retreats, but her tumor was not the only thing eating away at her. The anger she felt concerning her 23 year-old daughter, Melanie, was doing the same.

By all accounts, Melanie exhibited some pretty strong rebellious behavior. She was verbally abusive to Janet and her new husband, Jim, and she had attached herself to a rather unsavory man. "I hate her with a vengeance," Janet related. "Her behavior towards me and Jim is simply abominable, and I can't stand it any more. I really hate her."

We dug a little deeper into Janet's personal history and found that a similar relationship had existed between Janet and her own mother. It was not as clear and dramatic as

107

the drama with Melanie, but the dynamic was similar. Janet had resented how much her mother controlled her and tried to run her life. Janet did not rebel like Melanie, though. Instead, she became withdrawn and cold toward her mother.

We began to explore how the dynamic with Melanie reflected her soul's willingness to help her heal her issues with her mother, but Janet was not willing to see this. She simply was too angry to hear anything that did not correspond with her feelings. So, we asked her to move into her anger, to feel and to express it by beating cushions with a tennis racquet and shouting. (Anger is very effectively released through the combination of physical action and the use of the voice.) Although she released some anger toward her mother, her anger with Melanie remained.

Janet's *Satori*

That evening's retreat session was reserved for **Satori-Breath.** To experience Satori-Breath and use it for healing, everyone in the group lies on the floor and breathes consciously and vigorously for about an hour while listening to loud music. (See Part 4, Chapter 27.) While this may sound bizarre, breathing in this manner often results in emotional release, insight and integration of change at the cellular level. That night, Janet had her Satori — her awakening.

After the breathing session, people began sharing what had happened for them during the exercise. As soon as Janet began to share, we knew something important had happened.

Her voice was soft and sweet, whereas before it had been hard and abrasive. Her posture was relaxed and open, whereas before it had been tight and constricted. There was not a trace of the anger that had filled her being and which we all had felt emanating from her previously. She was calm and evidently peaceful. In fact, she hardly seemed the same person.

"I have no idea what all this means," she began. *"All I know is that I saw something while I was breathing, and it felt more real than anything I can possibly describe. Nothing much happened for quite a while after I began breathing,"* she continued. *"Then, suddenly I found myself floating in space, out there in the ethers. I was not in a body, and I knew with certainty that I was re-experiencing a time before I came into my current life. I was pure spirit. I have never felt so peaceful and calm. Then, I became aware of Melanie, also in spirit form. She came close, and we began to dance together — just dancing in space without limitation.*

"We began a conversation about coming into our next lifetime together," Janet said. *"This lifetime. The big question we had to decide was who would play what role — who was going to play the mother and who was going to play the daughter. It didn't much matter, for either way it was going to be a difficult assignment for us both. It would be a very strong test of our love. We had to decide, so we agreed that I would be the mother and she would be the daughter, and that we would incarnate soon thereafter. That's about it,"* she concluded.

109

"It doesn't sound like a whole lot happened, but really it did. I just can't put it into words. I just can't describe the depth and the meaning of what I experienced."

Energies Transformed

We discussed her experience and looked at the notion of mission as suggested by Janet's vision. Several others in the group felt strongly about her experience and saw parallels in their own lives. I suggested that Janet say nothing at all to Melanie when she returned home after the retreat. Within a few days of Janet's homecoming, Melanie called her mother and asked if she could come and talk. Janet agreed, and, while the first meeting was tentative and awkward, their relationship changed dramatically after that. Melanie soon dropped all her bizarre behavior, sent the unsavory boyfriend packing and came home to be with her mother and to take care of her during her illness. They literally became best friends and were quite inseparable after that. In addition, Janet's mother began calling more often, and gradually their relationship began to improve as well.

In this example, the transformation of energy happened in a roundabout way. Janet was extremely resistant to forgiving Melanie. Her soul guided her to the retreat so she could do a process that opened her to a remembrance of her mission agreement, which in turn, enabled her to see the perfection in the situation. By forgiving Melanie she transformed the hate in their relationship and, as a result, healed the original pain between herself and her mother.

Missions to Heal the Collective

While all of us come in to heal aspects of our own soul or those of our soul group, some may incarnate with a larger role to play. This may be to take on particular energies that get played out at the social/political/national and international level and offer large groups of people the opportunity to heal.

Of course, as with all missions, it may not look anything like a healing opportunity. It may show up as a war or a famine, or maybe a natural disaster. But when we open to the possibility that a group soul healing is being offered and that the whole thing is being orchestrated by Spirit for the greater good of all souls involved, we begin to see things very differently. Let me give you some seemingly outrageous examples.

1. Suppose the soul who came in to become Adolf Hitler came in with a mission to transform the victim consciousness of the Jewish race and the superiority consciousness of the German race.

2. What if Saddam Hussein came in to help American consciousness transform its guilt about slavery and the terrible abuse of its own people.

3. Suppose Slobodan Milosevic came in to enable America to project onto him the self-hatred it feels about the ethnic cleansing it has perpetrated against the Native American Indians.

111

4. What if the Chinese Government had to invade Tibet so that the Dalai Lama would be forced to travel the world and spread his beautiful message beyond the borders of Tibet.

5. Suppose the soul that was Princess Diana chose to die in exactly the way she did, and when she did, in order to open the heart chakra of England.

[In the first edition of this book Princess Diana's story appeared as the Epilogue. That was because she died within a very few days of my going to press so it had to go in almost as an afterthought. However, in this new edition, I am including it in this chapter since it is so pertinent to the issue of mission.

The event was still very fresh in my mind when I first wrote about Diana's death. The funeral had only just taken place and the emotional outpouring was still continuing. I was still very much in the experience of it all and I think that comes over in the piece. For that reason, I have decided to not alter the original version in any way so that you might experience the 'satori' vicariously through my own experience of it.]

Good-bye England's Rose

I began this book with a story about my sister Jill. The purpose of it was to illustrate how a seemingly desperate situation can be transformed when we approach it from the standpoint of Radical Forgiveness.

Just a few days before going to print, fate handed me an opportunity to end the book with a story that was equally instructive and open to a Radical Forgiveness perspective.

Unlike the one about Jill, this story was one with which virtually everyone in the world was familiar, as well as deeply involved emotionally. I refer of course to the story of Princess Diana who made her unexpected transition in the early hours of Sunday, August 31, 1997.

The drama began for me when my lifetime friend, Peter Jollyman, woke me with a phone call from England. For him it was around midday, but for me in Atlanta, it was still early and I had not yet seen a newspaper or listened to the radio. "Have you heard about the accident?" he asked. "What accident?" I replied, still in a stupor but aware enough to realize this had to be serious for him to be calling like this. "Princess Di was killed last night in a car crash in Paris. She was being chased by paparazzi. Her car spun out of control and hit a concrete post. She and Dodi were killed."

I noticed a perfunctory pang of remorse pass through me as I listened to the details as best he knew them at the time, but I can't say that it lasted more than a few moments. I tried to sound suitably shocked, but I really felt somewhat ambivalent about it.

Lot's of people died in the last 24 hours, I thought, after I put the phone down. Why would her death be any more, or any less, tragic than anyone else's. It was

113

her time to go and that's about all there is to it. Sad for her two boys though, of course. With that, I went downstairs to make tea and fix breakfast.

Then I turned on the TV and from that moment on, slowly began to get drawn into, and involved with, what was to become, in the days culminating in her funeral on Saturday morning, a roller-coaster of emotion.

As the days went by, I realized that something quite extraordinary was going on. The reaction to Princess Diana's death, not only in England, but throughout the world, was truly phenomenal. As I saw my country-men on the TV in heartfelt pain, crying and grieving in public — something English people simply do not do ordinarily — I found myself feeling the same emotions and crying with them. I was shocked to realize that I was hurting too. Somehow this woman, whom I had never met or thought much about, especially during the thirteen years I have lived in the U.S., had touched me deeply. I felt the loss profoundly and I was very surprised.

I really began to pay attention and to wonder what was really happening here. Something of extraordi-narily deep significance was occurring and I began an inner search to find the message and the meaning in it. Diana's death clearly had meaning far beyond the ap-parent circumstances in which it occurred, dramatic as they appeared to be. Some higher purpose was being played out here, I thought.

114

Then on Wednesday, it hit me. As I watched the scenes from England and experienced the great outpouring of emotion from people not in the least renowned for showing their emotions, especially in the open, I suddenly realized what Diana's spiritual mission had been. The over-arching purpose of her incarnation had been to open the heart chakra of Great Britain and by so doing, greatly accelerate the spiritual evolution of the British people, no less. I had no doubt whatsoever that she had achieved exactly that.

No one who watched the events of that week could ever doubt that she had single-handedly transformed the country — and indeed, much of the world — at the heart level. Only a very few people in all of human history come to mind as having had such an effect on the world purely through the expression of love energy: Gandhi, Martin Luther King and Nelson Mandela perhaps; Mother Teresa and Jesus Christ, certainly. (No wonder the Queen of England bowed her head to Diana's coffin — something never before witnessed.)

While in terms of human achievement and spiritual example in life, any comparison with Mother Teresa would be unfair; it is nevertheless interesting to note that the death of Mother Teresa, whose life and work, in most people's eyes, has brought her close to sainthood in her lifetime, did not take the spotlight off Diana even for a moment. That two women whose lives so deeply touched the world through authentic love should make their transitions within days of each other like this has enormous spiritual significance.

115

Even though the British people had been through two wars this century, suffering and grieving enormous losses, they came through it all with their legendary sense of humor and proverbial stiff upper lip, but not, I think it is fair to say, with an open heart. That had to wait, not only the coming of a people's princess, but her divinely planned, and to us at least, untimely and tragic death.

Since then, commentators have tried in vain to explain her effect on the world in terms of our fixation on, and willingness to almost deify, celebrities we know only through the media. Jonathan Alter in Newsweek came closer than most by referring to what Richard Sennett, in The Fall of Public Man, called the ideology of intimacy, in which people "seek to find personal meaning in impersonal situations." It is true that people did not know her personally and to that extent it remains an impersonal situation. Yet she transcended those limitations imposed by time and space and somehow touched everyone's heart very deeply in a way that cannot be easily explained.

The key to understanding her power as a human being lies in the archetype of the wounded healer, which teaches us that our power lies in our wounds — in the sense that it is the wound in me that evokes the healing in you and the wound in you that evokes the healing in me. We are all wounded healers but we don't know it. When we keep our wounds hidden and totally private, we separate from, and deny healing, not only

*to ourselves, but to countless others too. The stiff up-
per lip is a terrible way to withhold love. It atrophies
the heart and cripples the soul. Through her willingness to share her deepest wounds with the whole world,
Princess Diana evoked the healer in all of us, opened
our hearts and healed our fractured souls.*

*The whole world watched as people took their cue from
Diana and opened up, sharing their grief and their
woundedness, just as she had done. She gave the people
a language of intimacy that they could use to express
feelings openly and authentically. I don't recall seeing
one display of emotion and feeling that was not totally
authentic, and on television today that is indeed unusual.*

*As we each begin to emerge from behind the pain of
loss and the rope burns of grief, anger and projection
of guilt regarding our insatiable appetite for Diana's
image and curiosity about her life, which the press and
paparazzi merely reflected for us, we begin to discern,
through the mists and veils, the divine perfection of it
all. The more we contemplate the mission she accepted
and the extent to which she succeeded, the more we
are able to surrender into that perfection.*

*We find ourselves experiencing a new level of peace as
we move beyond the emotions and thoughts that once
would have tied us to the World of Humanity forever
and held us hostage to the victim archetype and move
towards the acceptance of the fact that it all had to*

unfold in exactly that way. The mission absolutely required the upbringing that she had, the marriage that went terribly wrong, the rejection she suffered at the hands of the royal establishment, the criticism of the press, the hounding by the paparazzi, the dramatic and violent death — everything, down to the very last detail.

And as the future unfolds, you will notice that now that Diana has returned 'home' having completed her mission, the energies that held all those dynamics in place will begin to disperse. Not only is she released from those dynamics, so are all the other people who were involved in the drama we know to be only an illusion. Charles is now free to become warmer, less distant and a more loving father to his two boys — and he undoubtedly will. (The Press will say that he changed because of what happened, but we will know the real truth.) The Queen will probably become less stuffy, more open and not quite so irrelevant. The monarchy itself will transcend the cult of personality and will become a stronger, more meaningful institution, not as a direct response to what happened, but because of the energy shift that occurred when the mission was over and the transformation complete.

But just because someone opens their heart chakra, there's no guarantee that they will keep it open. That remains a matter of choice at every moment. The same is true of the collective. The British people, and others around the world, will either stay in the love vibration

118

that Diana's death catapulted them into, and use that power to transform themselves, their royal family and their society, or they will focus on the illusion of what happened, blaming Charles, the royal family in general, the driver, the press and others. If they choose the latter, that will be their choice and perfect in its own way, but it will cause the collective heart chakra to close again.

Perhaps this book has a part to play in keeping the collective heart chakra open. Maybe the insight you have gained by reading it will enable you to remain focussed, not on the illusion of what happened in the tunnel that night in Paris, but on what is real in the Princess Diana story from beginning to end and the mission that gave it meaning and significance.

Maybe everyone who reads this book will truly recognize and acknowledge that, just as Jeff played his part for Jill in the story of Part One, Charles played his part beautifully for Diana — as did Camilla Parker-Bowles and the Queen. Maybe it will be clear to everyone who reads this book that the drama called for such loving, courageous souls to play those parts in exactly those ways and, let it be said, at great cost to themselves. (Charles' sacrifice for the sake of the opening of the heart chakra of Britain was absolutely no less than Diana's — in fact, in ordinary human terms, probably greater. It may have cost him his crown, no less!)

Maybe too, it will be obvious to everyone that it was all agreed in advance, prior to each character's soul

119

incarnating into this world and that the paparazzi were also playing an essential and loving part in all this too, as were the editors who paid for intrusive pictures of Diana.

Those who are indeed able to do the Radical Forgiveness reframe to this extent, recognizing that there were no victims here, will be a great beacon of light to all those who might otherwise choose to focus on the illusion, close their hearts and lose the love vibration. It is my fervent hope that every reader who is changed by my book will become a beacon of love — taking over where Diana left off, helping people stay in this new and higher vibration that her perfectly timed transition triggered.

*And it seems to me that you lived your life
like a candle in the wind:
never fading with the sunset
when the rain came in.
And your footsteps will always fall here,
along England's greenest hills;
your candle's burned out long before
your legend ever will.*

From © "Candle in the Wind," Polygram International, Inc. Written and performed by Elton John in Westminster Abbey at the funeral of Diana, Princess of Wales, September 6, 1997.

11: Transforming the Victim Archetype

A s we saw in the last chapter, our primary mission is to transform the victim archetype and raise the consciousness of the planet. But what does it mean to transform anything, and how does it raise consciousness?

The first thing to understand is that we can transform something only when we choose it as our spiritual mission. We make the decision about our mission not in this world but in the World of Divine Truth prior to incarnating.

The second thing to realize is that transforming something *does not* mean changing it. In fact:

To transform anything we must experience it fully and love it just the way it is.

For example, maybe your individual mission involved being born into an abusive family to experience the abuse first hand and to know it either as a victim or as a perpetrator. Remember, once you incarnate, your memory of your agreed-upon mission disappears. If you remembered your mission, you would not experience the energy and the feelings of victimhood as fully. Only in the experience of being victimized can you possibly come to realize what lies behind the illusion of victimhood — the projection of your guilt. If you are able to look beyond the illusion of the perpetrator and recognize these actions as a call for love, and if you respond with love and total acceptance, the victim energy is transformed and the consciousness of all involved is raised. In addition, the energy that holds the pattern of abuse disappears and the behavior stops immediately. That is what transformation is all about.

On the other hand, if we do not recognize the truth in the situation, or do not see beyond the illusion, and we try to change the physical circumstances, we lock up the energy that holds the pattern of abuse in place and nothing changes.

Only Love Transforms

Only love has the ability to transform energies like child abuse, corporate greed, murder and all other so-called evils of the world. Nothing else has any impact. Actions taken to change such situations, such as removing a child from an abusive environment, while humane in and of themselves, do not create transformation. The reason for this is simple: First, such action arises from fear, not love. Second, our intervention and our judgments maintain the energy pattern of abuse and lock them up more securely.

This explains why the decision to transform something can be made only from the World of Divine Truth. We humans are so locked into our beliefs about pain and suffering, fear and death, that even while we may believe that a particular child's soul came into this world to experience abuse and actually wants to feel abused, we simply cannot stand by and watch this happen. While the mission looks easy from the world of Divine Truth, it appears quite different down here on the physical plane. Who could possibly leave an abused child in an abusive environment? We cannot help but intervene. We are human!

And as we saw in an earlier chapter, we need to surrender to the idea that Spirit knows exactly what it is doing. If it were not in the child's highest and best interest for there to be an intervention on its behalf, it will set things up so that no one notices it. If on the other hand, Spirit decides an intervention is to the soul's highest good, it will arrange for it to occur. But this is not our decision. We, as human beings, must always respond in the way that seems most humane, most caring and compassionate, while at the same time knowing that Love is contained in the situation.

Radical Forgiveness Transforms

As humans, we are still not totally impotent in this regard, because we can transform the energy of something like child abuse by using Radical Forgiveness. If we truly forgive, in the radical sense, all those involved in the abusive situation, we definitely have an impact on the energy pattern. Ultimately, the child will have to forgive to finally change the pattern, but each time any of us, in any situation, whether we are personally involved or not, choose to see the perfection in the situation, we change the energy at once.

I was once asked to address the National Society of Mediators at their annual conference. I was only to have about

123

45 minutes and they were to be eating lunch at the same time as listening to me! I went early to listen in on their discussions in order to try to get a feel for their way of thinking. I determined that, in terms of background, about 50% of the attendees were lawyers and 50% were counselors and that their commitment to mediation left them fairly open minded and flexible in their approaches to problem solving.

For the first twenty minutes or so, I did my best to explain the concepts and assumptions underlying Radical Forgiveness. Then I drew the following diagram to represent the energetic relationship between them and their clients.

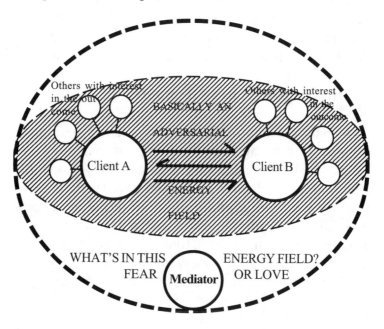

Fig. 9: Mediation Energy Fields.

I then put it to them that their perception of the situation they were mediating was likely to be that what was happening to Client A and B was unfortunate at best and a tragedy at worst. Also, that their role as mediator was to try to make the best of a bad job and resolve the situation in a way that would be the least damaging as possible to both parties and their dependents.

They agreed that this was a fair characterization of their task and that the energy field around the situation for the clients was one of hostility and mistrust. Had it been otherwise they wouldn't have needed a mediator. They concurred on this too.

Then I factored into the situation their own energy. They saw that their energy field would normally contain thoughts and feelings related to the perception that this was a 'bad' situation. I also suggested that, even though they were trying to mediate and help both clients, their perception of it being 'bad' fed into the client's energy field and reinforced their victim consciousness.

"What if," I asked then, "instead of seeing this situation as tragic and undesirable, you became willing to entertain the idea that this was a Divine plan unfolding exactly as it needed to unfold, and that each of the parties, including the ones on the periphery, were in actuality getting exactly what they subconsciously wanted at the soul level — and that this was true no matter how this situation worked out.

"Do you think that would make a difference? Your energy field, instead of being filled with fear-based thoughts and

125

emotions would be filled with love. Do you think that would have an effect on how the situation would finally become resolved?"

Surprisingly they understood. Even the lawyers got it! There was broad acceptance of the idea that how they held the situation in their own minds was a powerful factor in determining how the situation came out. It was not that anything would be done differently or overtly changed. It would just be that by them holding the idea that everything was perfect, the energy would be allowed to move, without as much resistance, in whatever direction it needed to move. That is what transforming energy means.

Morphic Resonance

What I have just described draws on Rupert Sheldrake's theory of morphic fields and morphic resonance. Sheldrake is an English biologist who postulates the existence of fields that are self-organizing and self-regulating systems in nature that organize and sustain patterns of vibratory or rhythmic activity. Elements are attracted to each other by morphic resonance to create these fields which are constantly changing and evolving. When one element in the field changes, this affects the whole field. The concept seems to be applicable at all levels, from quantum phenomena to social group behavior.

In the human context, morphic fields link individual members through extrasensory and energetic resonance (consciousness), a process that is independent of time and space. This is why, when someone forgives, the effect is felt immediately by the person being forgiven no matter how far away they are.

Returning to our situation with the mediators, we can think of the situation they most often find themselves in as a morphic field in which the individuals are being held together, through morphic resonance, by a victim consciousness. As soon as one member (the mediator) shifts his consciousness in the direction of love and acceptance of what is, as is, the field immediately undergoes a transformation and evolves into a new vibratory arrangement of a higher order. Through morphic resonance, the other members of the group have an opportunity to become realigned in the same way and for the situation to evolve on completely different lines to the way it would have had the consciousness not been transformed in this way.

I mention this particular research to show that the way we talk about energy and consciousness has a firm foundation in modern scientific research and theory.

Nelson Mandela Has Shown Us How

How Nelson Mandela handled the South African situation when apartheid finally ended in the early 1990s was an object lesson in how to transform energy through Radical Forgiveness. Apartheid, the white dominated political system in place for three-quarters of a century, kept blacks and whites separated — the whites in luxury and the blacks in terrible poverty. Mandela himself was imprisoned for 26 years. Upon his release he became President of the country. South Africa was ripe for a bloodbath of revenge, yet Mandela brought about an amazingly peaceful transition — the hallmark of which was not revenge but forgiveness.

It was not so much what he did that prevented the predicted bloodbath from occurring, but how he handled the energy. He refused to take revenge, and on behalf of all the people, he transcended the victim archetype. This, in turn, collapsed the energy pattern of potential violence already in place and waiting to be triggered. South Africa remains in transition today and not without problems, but its progress is far more than we could have dreamed possible a few decades ago.

Our collective mission to transform the victim archetype demands that we all follow Mandela's lead and move beyond the experience of victimhood. If we do not, we will stay hopelessly addicted to our woundedness and to the victim archetype.

Spirit Nudges

Deep inside our subconscious mind, we are in touch with our mission. Spirit keeps presenting opportunities to transform the victim energy by bringing things like incest, child abuse, sexual abuse, and racial hatred to the surface. Each one of us can embrace this mission by practicing Radical Forgiveness in any of these situations. If taken by enough of us, the shift in perception that allows us to see the perfection will transform the situation so the need for such energy patterns disappears.

Exercise in Transformation

To transform the victim archetype, practice the following:
Every time you watch the news, shift your consciousness
from one of judgment to one of seeing the perfection in the *radical!*
situation. Instead of accepting at face value a story about
racial prejudice, for example, help transform the energy of
racial disharmony. Do so by looking at the person or situation that would ordinarily receive your judgment and cen-
sure and see if you can move into a space of loving acceptance. Know that the people in the story are living out their
part in the Divine plan. Do not see anyone as a victim and
refuse to label anyone as a villain. People are just acting in
dramas being played out so healing can occur. *Remember, God does not make mistakes!*

12: The Ego Fights Back

By reminding us that we are spiritual beings having a human experience, Radical Forgiveness raises our vibration and moves us in the direction of spiritual evolution.

Such growth represents a real threat to the Ego (defined as the deep-seated, complex belief system that says we are separated from God and that He will one day punish us for choosing that). This is because the more spiritually evolved we become, the more likely it will be that we will remember who we are — and that we are one with God.

Once we have this realization, the Ego must die. If there is one thing we know about belief systems of any kind, they resist all attempts at making them wrong and the Ego is no exception. (People demonstrate all the time that they would rather be right than happy).

The more we use Radical Forgiveness therefore, the more the Ego fights back and tries to seduce us into remaining addicted to the victim archetype. One way it accomplishes this task is by using our own tools of spiritual growth. A good example of this is found in the Ego's use of *inner child work* to meet its own ends.

Inner child work gives us a way to look within ourselves and to heal the wounds of childhood we still carry within us as adults and that continue to affect our lives today.

However, the Ego sees an opportunity for its own survival in our focus on our woundedness. It exploits that kind of inner child work that uses the inner child as a metaphor for our woundedness to strengthen our attachment to the victim archetype. The behavior that this gives rise to is the constant revisiting of our wounds; giving them power through constantly speaking about them; projecting them onto a so-called inner child and using them as the means to finding intimacy.

Blaming Our Parents

Much of the inner child work of the eighties focused heavily on blaming our parents, or someone else, for the fact that we are unhappy now. The idea "I would be happy today if it weren't for my parents," is the mantra associated with this work. It gives us permission to feel that *they did this to us,* a perception that is much easier to live with than believing we have somehow *requested* to be treated in this manner. Such a viewpoint also pleases the Ego, because it automatically recreates us as victim. As long as we continue blaming our parents for our problems, each succeeding generation continues this belief pattern.

Clearing Emotional Toxicity

I do not wish to imply that getting in touch with our repressed childhood rage and pain and finding ways to

132

release it, is bad. In fact, doing so is essential. We must first do this work before moving onto forgiveness, for we cannot forgive if we are angry. However, too many workshops and therapies focus purely on our anger and fail to help us transform it through forgiveness of any kind. When we couple anger work with Radical Forgiveness, all sorts of repressed emotional and mental toxicity are cleared and the permanent release of anger becomes possible. Thus, we move out of woundedness and beyond victimhood.

Navaho Forgiveness Ritual

I once heard Caroline Myss describe the ritual that the Navaho Indians had for preventing woundology from becoming an addictive pattern. While they certainly recognized the need for people to speak of their wounds and to have them *witnessed* by the group, they understood that speaking about their wounds gave the wounds power, especially when done to excess. Therefore, if a person had a wound or a grievance to share, the tribe would meet and the person could bring it to the circle. This person was allowed to air his grievance three times and everyone listened with empathy and compassion. On the fourth occasion, however, as the person came into the circle, everyone turned their backs. "Enough! We have heard you express your concern three times. We have received it. Now let it go. We will not hear it again," they said. This served as a powerful ritual of support for letting go of past pain.

Imagine if we were to support our friends in that same manner? What if, after they had complained about their

133

wounds and their victimization three times, we then said, "I have heard you enough on this subject. It's time you let it go. I will not give your wounds power over you any longer by allowing you to talk about them to me. I love you too much."

I am sure if we did this, many of our friends would call us traitors. They would likely see our behavior not as an act of pure loving support but of betrayal and might turn against us immediately.

Being a True Friend

If we are to truly support each other in the journey of spiritual evolution, I believe we have no choice but to take the risk, draw a line in the sand with those we love and do our best to gently help move them beyond their addiction to their wounds. Such action will lead us to the achievement of our collective mission to transform the victim archetype and to remember who we really are.

13: Time, Medicine & Forgiveness

S piritual evolution brings with it a new appreciation for and knowledge of our physical bodies and how to care for them. The medical paradigm we have held for the last 300 years — ever since the French philosopher, Rene Descartes defined the body as a machine — is changing radically as it moves towards a holistic, mind-body approach.

We used to think of health as the absence of disease. Now, we think of health in terms of how well our *life-force* (prana, chi, etc), flows through our bodies. For optimum health this life-force must be able to flow freely. We cannot be healthy if our bodies are clogged with the energy of resentment, anger, sadness, guilt, and grief.

When we speak here of the body, we include not only the physical body, which is also an *energy body*, but the subtle bodies which surround us as well. These we refer to individually as the etheric body, the emotional body, the mental body, and the causal body. They each have a different frequency. Whereas we used to define our body in terms of chemicals and molecules, physicists have taught us how to see them as *dense condensations of interacting energy patterns.*

135

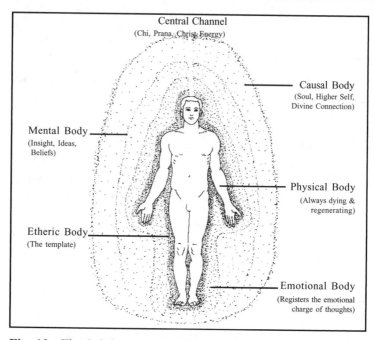

Fig. 10: The Subtle Energy Bodies

The subtle fields envelop the physical body in layers like vibrating sheaths of energy, each one an octave higher than the other. However, they are not fixed bands with clear boundaries as shown in the diagram above. Rather, they are, to a large degree, diffused within the same space as if they were all part of an ocean of energy surrounding our bodies. The subtle bodies are not so much defined by their position in space as by the different frequencies at which they vibrate.

The subtle bodies resonate harmonically with the vibrating patterns of the physical body, enabling consciousness (mind)

136

to interact with the body. This is what we mean when we speak of the *body-mind continuum,* with mind existing both inside and outside the physical body. (For more details on the qualities and purpose ascribed to each of these subtle bodies, refer to Part 3, Chapter 15)

Clogged Filters Stress the Furnace

To ground this concept in a practical analogy, think of our bodies as being like the filters typically found in home heating furnaces — the kind we have to clean from time to time to ensure the furnace works efficiently. Just as these filters were designed to allow air to move easily through them, the same is true of our bodies. Life-force must be free to flow easily through all our bodies — our physical body and our subtle bodies, too.

Whenever we judge, make someone wrong, blame, project, repress anger, hold resentment, etc., we create an energy block in our body/bodies. Each time we do this, our filter becomes a little more blocked and less energy remains available for our *furnace.* Sooner or later the filter fails, and starved of the vital oxygen it must have to keep burning, the *flame* dies. More simply, when our physical and subtle bodies become too clogged for life-force to flow through easily, our body starts shutting down. In many cases, this manifests first as depression. Eventually, our body gets sick, and, if the blocks are not removed, we may die.

You may recall how my sister Jill felt a release of energy when she moved into Radical Forgiveness. Her life-force filter was blocked by her toxic belief system about her own lack of worthiness, not to mention past resentments, anger, sadness, and frustrations over her current situation. When she let all that go, her energy blocks were cleared, which allowed her to shift her emotional state as well. Whenever you *forgive radically*, you release enormous amounts of life-force energy that then can be made available for healing, creativity and expressing your true purpose in life.

Farra's Flu Release

My good friend Farra Allen, co-founder of the Atlanta School of Massage and a mind-body counselor, took ill with a particularly virulent strain of flu that typically kept people in bed for 10 days or more. It hit him hard, but instead of giving all his power to the virus, he decided to do some inner work around it, work that might shift the energy pattern holding the virus in place. Using a process known as *active imagination*, which simply involves writing down thoughts as a *stream of consciousness*, he came upon a hitherto unconscious and unresolved emotional issue. He used Radical Forgiveness to clear the issue, and the flu disappeared almost immediately. He was working full-time and feeling great within two days of the onset of his illness. This was a powerful demonstration of the healing power of Radical Forgiveness.

Will Cancer Respond Too?

Suppose the illness had been cancer rather than the flu and it was our belief that it started as a deeply-repressed emotion. Thinking the cure lay in releasing that energy block, our recommendation might have been that my friend get in touch with the repressed feelings, feel them fully and then let them go.

However, unlike Farra's flu attack, which probably moved from his subtle body into his physical body in just a few days, this energy pattern might have taken many years to move from the subtle body into the physical body and, in time, to manifest as a disease. The question that haunts us then becomes, *'How long will it take for the disease process to fully reverse itself using emotional release work alone?'* Conceivably, it could require the same number of years it took for the disease to manifest — not very practical if you have cancer or some other disease where time is of the essence — or so it might seem, anyway.

Time Is a Factor In Healing

We used to think of time as something fixed and linear until Einstein proved that time actually is relative and that consciousness becomes a factor in the equation. The more elevated our consciousness, the faster we evolve and the faster things happen with regard to change in any physical matter to which we give attention.

Think of consciousness as our vibratory rate. It would probably take far too long to reverse the disease process of cancer energetically if we possess a low vibratory rate. It automatically will be low if we are in fear, hold anger and resentment in our beingness, think of ourselves as a victim, and/or have our energy locked up in the past. For the majority of us, this represents our consciousness most of the time. Therefore, few of us could reverse a disease like cancer fast enough relying solely on releasing the emotional cause of the disease — that is, unless we found a way to raise our vibratory rate.

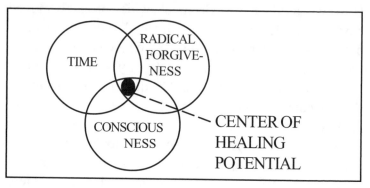

Fig. 11: Time & Healing.

By letting go of the victim archetype and bringing our energy into present time through the process of Radical Forgiveness, we might raise our vibration enough to create at least a quicker, if not immediate, disease reversal. We improve our chances if we also incorporate other ways of raising our vibration, such as prayer and meditation.

Example: A lady who attended one of our retreats had had several surgeries for ovarian cancer and had just been given by her doctors, at most, three months to live. She was depressed and had little life-force left. She said she only really came to the retreat because the people in her church had collected the money for her to come, so she felt obliged to do so. We worked with her and on the third day had a wonderful breakthrough that put her in touch with an event that occurred when she was 2 1/2 years old and had made her believe herself to be utterly worthless. She released a lot of emotion around that issue and grieved for the countless number of times she had created her life in ways that proved her worthless. After that, her life-force energy increased. By the time she left she was all fired up to find an alternative program that would help her beat the cancer and the doctor's prognosis. She was even willing to travel outside the USA if the method she chose was illegal in this country. (Many are illegal in the USA.) After two weeks of frantically searching for the treatment to which she felt most drawn, she suddenly realized that her healing would come through prayer. So, she went away to a place in upstate New York and worked with a couple who offered prayer-weeks. She literally prayed for a week. Upon her return, she went to her oncologist who examined her and said, "I don't know how to explain this, but you have absolutely no cancer in your body. I could say it was a spontaneous remission, but I believe in God and I am not willing to describe it in any other way than as a miracle."

This woman serves as a wonderful example of how raising the vibration through prayer reversed the physical condition in days rather than years. I believe that Radical Forgiveness would have done the same.

Seattle Forgiveness Study

An interesting, but as yet unpublished, study on forgiveness and time was conducted at Seattle University in WA.

It involved a series of interviews with people who, by their own assessment, had been victimized. The researchers wanted to see how that perception changed over time. Preliminary findings showed that serenity, which was described as "having no resentment left," came NOT through any act of forgiveness but as a sudden *discovery* that they had forgiven. All reported that the more they tried to forgive, the harder it became and the more resentment they felt. They stopped trying to forgive and *just let go.* After varying intervals of time came the surprising realization that they no longer harbored resentment and that they had, in fact, forgiven.

A later, and even more interesting, discovery revealed that the realization that they had forgiven was preceded by being forgiven themselves. (Who forgave them and for what was irrelevant.) However, what this certainly points to is that forgiveness is a shift in energy. Having experienced being forgiven — a release of stuck energy — they were able to release their own stuck energy with someone else.

This study not only reinforces the insight that forgiveness cannot be willed but also shows that forgiveness happens as an internal transformation through a combination of surrendering one's attachment to resentment and accepting forgiveness for oneself.

Additionally, this study's results underscore the value of Step Nine in the Twelve-Step process used successfully by millions of people in Alcoholics Anonymous and other similar programs. Step Nine asks that we seek to make amends with those we have harmed and that we ask those people for forgiveness. When we find that we have in fact been forgiven, this frees our own energy to forgive not only others but ourselves as well.

Time Heals - Fast or Slow

Some might argue that the Seattle study illustrates the slowness of the forgiveness process and shows that forgiveness would offer a rather ineffective method for curing a disease such as cancer. In many cases, it took people decades to discover they had forgiven.

The important distinction to make, however, is that the study did not distinguish between Radical Forgiveness and traditional forgiveness. What it described was definitely the latter. I would be willing to wager that, if the subject group had been divided into two — one group with insight into Radical Forgiveness and the other left basically to use traditional forgiveness, the group with the additional insight would have reached the serenity state infinitely more quickly than the other group.

I am not claiming that Radical Forgiveness always occurs instantaneously either — though I have to say I have seen it happen instantaneously many times now. Neither can it be claimed as a definitive *cure* for cancer. However, it certainly should be an integral part of any treatment protocol. Sometimes people delay medical treatment to see if Radical Forgiveness creates enough of an effect to make such drastic intervention unnecessary. That would be unthinkable with traditional forgiveness.

Mary's Story

My friend Mary Pratt, a co-facilitator at many of my retreats denied for months that something was terribly wrong
with her health. When she could not ignore the obvious
any longer, she went to a doctor who told her she had
stage three colon cancer. They wanted to operate immediately. She asked them for 30 days, and they reluctantly
agreed. She went to a little cabin in the mountains and
stayed there for a week, meditating and working on forgiving all the people in her life, including herself, using Radical Forgiveness. She fasted, prayed, cried, and literally
went through *the dark night of the soul*. She came back
home and worked with several practitioners to cleanse her
body and strengthen her immune system.

At the end of the 30-day period, the surgery was performed. Afterwards, the doctor wanted to know what she
had done, for the cancer had all but disappeared and instead of the radical surgery they had said would be necessary, removal of the cancer required only minor intervention.

Buying Time

In cases where the disease is so advanced or aggressive
as to require immediate medical intervention, surgery, chemotherapy or radiation buys time. In that sense, such treatment becomes not only helpful but, at times, necessary.

Remember, there is no cure for cancer. Consequently, no
matter what the medical treatment, the doctor's have an

unspoken expectation that a recurrence is almost a for-gone conclusion and just a question of time. I prefer to look at the treatment, assuming the patient survives it, as a way to buy the time to do the Radical Forgiveness work that could actually prevent any recurrence.

Preventive Medicine

Radical Forgiveness provides one of the best preventive measures available. Radical Forgiveness clears the energy in the subtle bodies long before it becomes a block in the physical body. When I help people resolve forgiveness issues by using Radical Forgiveness Therapy, like I did with my sister Jill, I believe I am not only helping them heal a wound in their subtle body, I am helping them prevent disease occurring in the physical body. I am convinced that if we keep the energy flowing in our bodies as it was designed to do, we never will get sick. Though I no longer do the 5-day cancer retreats, I nevertheless regard the Radical Forgiveness workshops that I now present all around the world as cancer prevention workshops.

Of course, adequate exercise, good diet and other such common sense practices help in this regard as well. However, keeping our energy bodies clear of emotional dross and toxicity is of primary importance to good health and healing. Unfortunately, this aspect of healing gets the least media attention despite the fact that, in America alone, one out of every five people takes an antidepressant drug like Prozac. Bearing in mind that depression always precedes cancer, we have to wonder whether it is mere coincidence that one out of five Americans also dies of cancer.

Forgiveness and Cancer

I am often asked why I work with people who have cancer. I have had no personal experience with it, and I knew little about it from a medical standpoint when I began offering five-day cancer retreats for emotional and spiritual healing in the early 1990's.

It was only after doing this for some time that I realized why I was attracted to this work. It was because it linked up with my interest with forgiveness. That insight occurred when I discovered that nearly all cancer patients, besides having a lifetime habit of suppressing and repressing emotions, are known to share a marked inability to forgive.

I now believe that lack of forgiveness contributes to, and may even be a principal cause of, most cancers. Therefore, my healing work with cancer patients, and with those who want to prevent the disease from arising or reoccurring in their bodies, now centers almost entirely on Radical Forgiveness Therapy.

Jane's Story

Jane came to one of our five-day retreats in the North Georgia mountains. She had had a mastectomy and was awaiting a bone-marrow transplant. After the retreat, she came to me once a week for hypnotherapy and individual coaching. On the second visit she arrived in a distressed state, because a routine Magnetic Resonance Imaging (MRI) scan had that day discovered minute spots of cancer in her brain. While this new cancer was upsetting enough by itself, its appearance also was liable to spoil her chances of a transplant. The doctors planned to give her chemotherapy to try and arrest the cancer's progress. However, they were surprised at her condition, because normally metastasis proceeds from the breast to the liver and then to the brain. Very rarely does cancer proceed directly from the breast to the brain. To me, this seemed worthy of some exploration.

Jane, an attractive woman in her early forties, had not been involved in a romantic relationship for about seven years. She had a boyfriend of sorts, but she described the relationship as not much more than a close friendship. In fact, she said she looked upon him as her *buddy,* even though she had sex with him from time to time. As I probed further into her relationship situation, she got in touch with some incredible grief she still felt around a relationship she had ended a number of years ago. This eight-year relationship was extremely passionate and intense, and Jane clearly worshipped the man. Four years into this relationship, which she believed was soon to be consummated in marriage, she discovered that he was married already and had children. He had no intention of leaving his wife. Jane was devastated but could not stop seeing him. It took her another four extremely painful years to extricate herself from this relationship.

It was clear to me, that as a result of this failed relationship, Jane had shut down her emotions completely and would no longer allow herself to get involved so deeply

147

with a man. Neither was I surprised that she had suffered a broken heart; most women with breast cancer have a broken heart somewhere in their history. (The breast is the organ of nurturance and is in the proximity of, and related to the heart.)

As she was going out the door at the end of our session, Jane said in a whisper, "I put him in the attic."

I stopped in my tracks. "What do you mean?" I asked.

"Well, everything I had accumulated over the years that had any connection to this man, or that would remind me of him, I stuffed in a box. I then put the box up in the attic. It's still there. I haven't touched it since."

I told her to sit down and tell me that again. I had her repeat the same thing three times. Suddenly, she saw the connection between the box in the attic that represented her broken love affair and her brain cancer. "Oh, my God," she said. "That's him in my head, isn't it? He's in my attic."

I told her to go home, go up into the attic and take down the box. I told her to bring it with her to her next session, and we would go through it piece by piece. We planned for her to tell me the story around each item until we had exorcised his energy and released the pain that she had repressed. Jane understood that this might be the key to her healing and was very excited. Tragically, she had a seizure the next day and was taken back to the hospital. She died a month later without ever touching the box in the attic. Looking at the box's contents and feeling the pain of her lost love may have been just too much for her to bear, and I feel, at some level, she may have decided to let go of life rather than face the pain.

Origins of Illness

Energy blocks always begin in the subtle bodies first. Then, if they are not released at that level, they move into the physical body and ultimately manifest as diseases such as cancer, multiple sclerosis, diabetes, and the like. Thus, we can say that illness always begins in the subtle bodies first and moves inward.

We used to think that the best way to stay ahead of disease was to visit a medical doctor for a regular checkup. We now know that we are much better off having a consultation with someone who can read our aura — meaning that they can tune into the energy patterns of our subtle bodies, particularly the etheric body. They can see blocks building energetically long before they show up in the physical body. Medical intuitives can do the same.

There are now also sophisticated technological diagnostic systems that do this. Called Electro-Dermal Screening Devices, they are mostly used by naturopaths, homeopaths, osteopaths and chiropractors. The machine uses the acupuncture points (which are in the etheric body), to get readings on each organ system of the body and to register disease at the subclinical level. These are proving to be very accurate devices, though as yet, most medical doctors fail

149

to recognize them. Healing a disease pattern in the subtle body proves much easier than waiting for it to condense into physical matter, because once it does that, it becomes much more resistant to change.

Emotional Garbage

Quantum physicists have actually proven that emotions condense as energy particles, which, if not expressed as emotion, become lodged in the spaces between atoms and molecules. That literally is the filter becoming clogged. Once the emotion has become a particle, it becomes much more difficult to release, and therein lies the problem. It takes much more time and effort to release that block from the physical body than it would have if it had been released while still in pure energy form in the subtle body/bodies — in this case the emotional body.

However, shifting those particles before they do harm is possible, and the best way I know to do so involves a combination of Radical Forgiveness and Satori-Breathwork. (See Part 4, Chapter 27). However, if those particles are left to accumulate and coagulate into a mass that one day becomes a cancer, the problem becomes highly intractable and, subsequently, life-threatening.

Why We Don't Heal

Clearly, time and healing are directly related. For us to evolve to the extent that we can heal ourselves, we must have most of our consciousness in present time — not in the past, not in the future, but in the *now*. Caroline Myss, in her tape series, "Why People Don't Heal," maintains that people with more than 60 percent of their life energy siphoned off to maintain the past are unable to heal themselves energetically. Thus, they remain totally reliant upon chemical medicine for their healing.

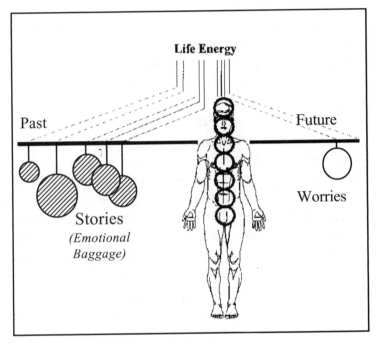

Fig. 12: Why People Don't Heal

She argues that if it takes 60 to 70 percent of the average person's precious life-force to manage the negative experiences of his or her childhood, adolescence and earlier years of adulthood, as well as to hold on to the losses, disappointments and resentments of the past, and another

10 percent worrying about, planning for and trying to control the future, that leaves precious little energy for the present moment — or for healing. (It is important to note that it does not drain our energy to maintain positive memories nor even negative memories if they have been processed and forgiven.)

Life has its own way of bringing us — and our energy — into present time. Often it is through trauma. When we find ourselves in the midst of a disaster, have an unexpected accident or discover that our lives suddenly are in danger, we become very focused on the present moment. We bring all our consciousness into the present instinctively. Suddenly, the past does not matter. The future does not matter. Only this moment exists. The power of such currently-focused energy is demonstrated when a mother, seeing her child trapped under a car, suddenly becomes able to lift the car off the ground so her child can be rescued. Acts of incredible bravery and courage also happen when energy becomes focused in the moment, because fear only occurs when we bring the past into the future. When we are truly in the moment we are absolutely fearless, because we have no awareness of past or future.

Radical Forgiveness helps us be in present time, because we do not *forgive radically* by going back into the past. We simply forgive the person who happens to be mirroring our projection right here in the present. That is the beauty of Radical Forgiveness. It is true that sometimes the past connection will be so clear, as in Jill's case, it illuminates the current situation. However, the focus is still on the perfection of what is happening *in the now*.

We can either choose to let go of the victim archetype and bring our energy into the present through Radical Forgiveness or wait for a significant trauma to force us into the now. In other words, we can either transform our consciousness as a matter of will, or we can wait for a disaster or a life threatening illness to make us do it.

14: As Above — So Below

Humanity as a whole could soon be faced with the same choice confronting each one of us as individuals. As was pointed out in the previous chapter, the choice is to heal by choice or trauma.

Heal by Choice or Trauma

Many visionaries claim that all the signs are present that point toward humankind receiving a massive demonstration of the *heal by choice or trauma principle* in the very near future.

The Earth has a cancer and it is called the human race. This living, breathing, conscious planet has been in a state of perfect balance its entire life with every little part doing what it must to sustain the system in balance. This is analogous to the job done by healthy cells in the human body.

For millions of years we have been part of that balanced system. In the last few thousand years, however, we have put ourselves above the natural order and have come to believe that we can control and dominate the entire system. Just as a cancer cell multiplies out of control, metastasizes throughout the system and begins to devour its host, so we continue to multiply exponentially out of control all

155

over the planet and to plunder its natural resources as if nothing else mattered beyond the satisfaction of our greed.

Like a tumor wrapping itself around the heart or blocking a lung, so do we, in the same kind of deadly embrace with our own life-source, chop down forests, pollute the very air that we breathe and poison the environment. The scientists are telling us that we are close to destroying life as we know it within the next 40-50 years if we don't make dramatic changes.

The greatest need however is for a change in consciousness. Collectively, we must change mass consciousness or face unprecedented trauma at such a level that all the existing structures maintaining our present life-style will be swept away.

Earth Changes and Political Upheaval

From earliest times right up to the present time, massive and disastrous Earth changes have been predicted for the early years of the new millennium. Predictions include two polar shifts, dramatic earthquakes, drastically-altered weather patterns, volcanic eruptions, and a significant rise in sea levels as polar ice-caps melt. The result of such events would be a radically changed map of the world with much of what we see today as land disappearing under water and new continents rising from the sea. The resulting disruption and chaos would be unimaginable and millions of people would die. Political upheavals, religious wars and environmental damage would also occur on a massive scale.

Such predictions were most notably made by the famous *seer* of the 16th century, Nostra Damas, and in this century by Edgar Cayce, the *sleeping prophet,* who made very precise predictions in the 1940's. They also appear in many religious writings, including the Bible's Book of Revelations and in the traditional texts of the Mayans, the Hopi Indians and many other spiritually-aware indigenous peoples.

It is clear to many that these *earth changes* have already begun. As the effects of global warming become impossible to ignore, the scientific community is making its own series of predictions based on the worldwide increase in floods, droughts, hurricanes, tornadoes, and volcanic eruptions, all of which bear close resemblance to the predictions of Cayce and others. Just recently the world has become a whole lot more unstable politically and some of what is happening looks uncomfortably like what has been predicted.

Consciousness Counts

The scientists do not talk much about the effects of consciousness on the earth, preferring instead to focus on what action we should take to prevent impending doom. However, the more spiritually-oriented predictions always have carried with them the caveat that the severity of the earth changes and the political upheaval may be mitigated to the extent that we human beings come to our senses and change our consciousness. In other words, even though our fear/greed-based consciousness has wounded the etheric body of the planet so badly that a violent eruption in its physical

157

form seems inevitable, we still can lessen the effect by raising our consciousness. Just as we have learned that a disease pattern in the etheric body of a human being can be healed by nonphysical means (prayer, Reiki, imagery, hands-on-healing, Radical Forgiveness, etc.), so the pattern of upheaval and violent change already set in the Earth's etheric body similarly can be dissipated before it manifests in the physical. The answer therefore seems to be, amazingly enough, prayer.

The Power of Prayer

Science has been putting the spotlight on prayer over the last few years and there is a growing consensus amongst that community that it actually works. We truly create our reality through our prayers. Not the kind of prayers, I hasten to add, that consist of requests or demands that God gives us this or that, or make this happen rather than that or in some other way tells God what to do.

No, the essence of creative prayer is not a matter of words or thoughts. It is actually *feeling*. Prayer will manifest what you want only when you are able to be fully in the feeling of having it already, knowing that it is done or that you have already been gifted with it. A feeling of profound gratitude is perhaps the nearest one can come in describing it.

But even this is tied to a particular outcome and probably will not raise the consciousness sufficiently high to shift the energy to the degree required.

The purest form of prayer we can engage in is to feel peace; the kind of peace that comes when we surrender totally to what is - as is — in the knowledge and comfort that Spirit has it all handled and that it will all work out for the best if we just get ourselves out of the way.

It is only when we are fully surrendered to the situation that we have now that the energy will open up for changes to occur — and what they will be, heaven only knows! Don't pray *for* peace. Pray to *feel* peace. That's the most creative prayer you can make. Peace is the strongest power on Earth and it is certainly called for at this time. When we can feel peace in our hearts, we will know Love and our world will reflect it.

This means that we have a choice. Each individual can make a choice to stay in the feeling of fear, lack, mistrust, greed and guilt or choose to let go of all that and be in peace. It is as simple as that. Peace/Love is the only antidote to the fear based consciousness that we now live in and participate in daily. So simply choose it. We have the technology. Use Radical Forgiveness daily in order to make that choice real — and see what happens!

Healing Crisis

What we may be seeing at this time is the Earth and all of Humankind going through a healing crisis — and it may have to get worse before it gets better. (A healing crisis occurs when an organism goes through what looks like a dramatic worsening of its condition, such as with a fever or an eruption of boils, just before it starts to get well again.

159

This worsened condition serves as a cleansing and detoxification process.)

All in Divine Order

No matter how drastic things get, we must believe that there is perfection and Divine purpose even in this kind of situation. After all, who could possibly have imagined a more dramatic way for Spirit to lovingly mirror our own lust for control and greed than this? Or to mirror our need to create separation between people? We cannot evolve spiritually while holding onto these energies, and if it takes Earth changes to bring us to a healing of them, so be it. The planet will be healed in the process. So too will we.

Focus on the Perfection

To put this whole discussion in perspective we must also keep in mind that, since the physical world actually is an illusion, what we experience as Earth changes will be illusionary, too. That explains why a change in human consciousness can change the situation immediately. How we experience Earth changes depends upon our perception of what is happening. If we see it as a purification of consciousness and a healing crisis that will result in a spiritual transformation, our experience of it will be in stark contrast to what we will feel if we take the victim position and think of it as real, as something to be feared and as a punishment for our rank stupidity. A Radical Forgiveness perspective will enable us to stay focused on the perfection of what is happening in the moment and will carry us through to the joy and peace on the other side of the experience.

The Gift

The adage *as above — so below* is meaningful too in terms of how we respond to both the cancer in our bodies and the cancer on the planet. Waging *war* on cancer with toxic drugs and other *violent* treatment will never bring about a cure for cancer. Violent, high-tech, politically motivated solutions to the Earth's problems won't work either. The only thing that will work, in both cases, is *Love.* When we really comprehend this, we will have understood the gift of both Earth changes and cancer.

No lesson is more crucial than this one. People with cancer are brave souls come to the physical plane with a mission to demonstrate the futility of projecting anger and war on the body and on ourselves. Their mission is to help us understand that the only answer to any situation is *Love.* Our gift in return is to hear their loving message.

Visions of Joy, Harmony and Peace

Whether or not we raise our vibration sufficiently to prevent trauma and come into loving resonance with all of life voluntarily, the end result ultimately will be the same. All the predictions about Earth changes speak of a breakthrough in consciousness happening in the wake of the Earth cleansing itself and balancing the karma we have created. Visions of life after the Earth changes being wonderfully harmonious, peaceful and idyllic, in stark contrast to the way it is today, is a common theme running through many of the predictions. Like all healing opportunities, we can heal our soul pain at the first sign of the repressed pain

161

occurring, or wait until it takes a disaster to wake us. However the Earth changes occur and at whatever level of destruction the planetary karma plays out, the changes will constitute the ultimate healing crisis for the planet and all of us. That will certainly be in Divine order.

Raising our vibration enough to change the predictions must include living our lives based on love and gentle acceptance of ourselves and others, forgiving ourselves for abusing the planet, and joining in prayer for peace with as many people as possible from around the world involved and embracing Radical Forgiveness as nothing less than a permanent way of life.

Postscript: *If this topic has interested you and you would actually like to be involved in creating this paradigm shift, using the Radical Forgiveness technology along with thousands of other people, then I might suggest you visit my web site and click on "America's Healing." Healing the soul of America could be the first step to awakening humanity.*

C.T. July, 2003.

PART THREE

Assumptions Expanded

15: Articles of Faith

The assumptions listed in Chapter Two were made briefly to give you just enough of an understanding of them to comprehend the theory of Radical Forgiveness. Now I would like to discuss in greater depth any assumptions underlying Radical Forgiveness that heretofore have not been comprehensively discussed. Hopefully, this will help you find a level of comfort with them, even if you cannot accept them totally.

Remember, all theories are based upon assumptions, but not all assumptions are proven with evidence of their validity. This holds especially true when dealing with theories and assumptions pertaining to the nature of reality and spiritual issues.

Interestingly, science and mysticism have come to a new level of agreement about the nature of reality and other spiritual questions that until now have seemed beyond the reach of science. For centuries, Hindu mystics have claimed to possess a *direct knowing* of these universal truths, which they claim to have arrived at as a result of 40 years of meditating in Himalayan caves. By using rigorous scientific methods and theoretical constructs, scientists recently have arrived at the same truths — or, should we say, have made similar assumptions. It is now safe to say that quantum physics actually demonstrates the truth of what the mystics have known for centuries. How exciting it is to see a joining of these two distinct ways of approaching and arriving at truth. Science and spirituality have come together at last with scientists becoming modern day mystics!

Yet, in spite of the progress we have made, in all humility we must continue to keep in mind that these assumptions, by their very nature, do not represent *the whole truth*. The great mystery of how the universe works and of the higher purpose of human life still seems to lie beyond mere mortal understanding, and it seems the assumptions we make are mere approximations of what might be the truth. On this basis, therefore, the following assumptions are given as the foundation for Radical Forgiveness.

Assumption: **Contrary to most Western religious thought, we are not human beings having an occasional spiritual experience. Rather we are spiritual beings having a human experience.**

This is not just a play on words. It represents a fundamental shift in our thinking about who we are and our relationship with God. Instead of thinking of ourselves as fallen and separated from God, it suggests that we are still very much connected to the All That Is and that life in a physical body is just a temporary interlude taken for the purpose of learning and balancing energy. It also suggests that God lives within each of us rather than *up there*, highlighting our dual *man/spirit* nature. Pulitzer Prize winner, Ernst

Becker, explained this vividly by saying, "Man is a God who shits."*

Phenomenal power exists in the idea that we are spiritual beings having a human experience. It represents a direct threat to the Ego, which consists of a cluster of beliefs that convince us we have separated from God and are subject to His wrath for committing that original sin of separation. If we, indeed, are not separate at all but totally connected, the Ego ceases to exist.

Assumption: **We have physical bodies that die, but we are immortal.**

For centuries philosophers have debated the makeup of the "soul." This discussion predates even Plato and Socrates, both of whom had much to say about the soul but remained very much at odds on the subject. Today, the debate continues with little agreement on what constitutes the soul.

For the purposes of this discussion, however, the soul is defined as that part of us that is pure consciousness connected to the greater ocean of consciousness that forms the All That Is. Yet, for the purposes of our incarnation, the soul takes on an individual characteristic that can be likened to a single droplet of that same ocean or a little bit of *God Stuff.* Since we are a part of the ocean of The All That Is, we have always existed as a soul. The soul has no beginning and no end, exits outside of both time and space

*Becker. E. *"The Denial of Death"* MacMillan Free Press, 1973,

and is immortal. During our incarnation, the soul keeps us connected to the World of Divine Truth and the All That Is and is responsible for our spiritual evolution.

Once the soul incarnates, it becomes attached to both a body and a personality, which together represent a *persona* or identity. This we create for ourselves based on our own self-concept, which we present to the world at large. Thus, our soul becomes subject to the stresses of human existence and can even become sick. A great many of the sicknesses of today, such as cancer, begin as a deep sickness of the soul. Shamans speak of the soul becoming fractured and splintered, parts of it actually being left behind and lost in past events, especially traumas. A great deal of a shaman's healing work revolves around the idea of soul retrieval.

Whether a soul incarnates just once or does so over and over again has been an issue of contention through the ages, and many churches and religions will not consider this idea even today. Yet, Eastern religions have always included reincarnation among their spiritual beliefs. I do not regard reincarnation as central to Radical Forgiveness and it is of no consequence whether one believes it or not. It has no effect on the efficacy of Radical Forgiveness and is simply a matter of personal choice. ***If the idea of reincarnation offends you, skip the next couple of pages.***

For myself, I am not attached either way though there does seem to be evidence to support the idea, especially through the vast amount of writing about near-death-experiences.

These accounts are so similar in their content and quality they hardly can be refuted. Thousands of people have reported similar kinds of experiences and exhibit the same kind of certainty that what they saw was real. The effect near death experiences have on their lives are more or less identical as well.

From this same source, it appears that not only do our souls incarnate numerous times but that they do not come into this physical life experience alone. Past life research seems to suggest that our souls keep coming back time and time again with others from our soul group to resolve particular *karmic* imbalances.

During our journey towards wholeness, we create energy imbalances that have to be restored. These imbalances are referred to as our karma. For example, if we take advantage of people and cheat them, we must at some time have the experience of being cheated to equalize the energy. This is not a moral exercise; it has nothing to do with right or wrong. As we have already noted, the Universe is neutral. This happens simply as a balancing of energy and is dictated by the Law of Cause and Effect, which states that for every action there must be an equal reaction. (See Chapter 9.)

The people with whom we play and the games we play with them are all about balancing energy in this manner. Our soul heals and becomes whole again each time we rebalance the karmic energies. Thus, each incarnation contributes to the healing of the soul.

Incidentally, since time does not exist in the world of Divine Truth, all our incarnations happen simultaneously. As we heal in one lifetime, we heal all the other incarnations as well. Use of Radical Forgiveness in one lifetime, therefore, provides incredible value to a soul, because it heals all the other incarnations at the same time as it heals the current one. Imagine the collective karma that was balanced by Nelson Mandela forgiving a whole generation of whites in South Africa for their treatment of blacks. By the same token, imagine the collective karma that remains to be balanced in America for the treatment of slaves and the Native American Indians.

Our Soul always moves us in the direction of healing and keeps creating situations that offer us the opportunity to balance karmic energy. However, if this healing is not accomplished at the level of Divine Truth, we tend to recreate the imbalance through the resentment and revenge cycle and the maintenance of victim consciousness. This keeps the wheel of karma spinning round and round and round. Radical Forgiveness provides one of the best ways to stop the wheel from turning, because it breaks the cycle.

Having said all that, if you have a problem with the concept of reincarnation, simply ignore it. It makes no difference.

Assumption: **While our bodies and our senses tell us we are separate individuals, in truth we are all one. We all individually vibrate as part of a single whole.**

We are not our bodies. We are not our Egos. We are not our personality selves or the roles we play each day. Believing we are these things serves to further reinforce our belief in separation. Upholding this belief makes it impossible for us to remember who we really are — an individual soul created as part of God and existing in oneness with God.

Assumption: **When all our souls were one with God, we experimented with a thought that separation was possible. We became trapped in that thought, which became the illusion or dream that we now live. It is a dream because the separation did not actually happen. We only think it did — and that thought gave birth to the belief system we call the Ego.**

Once we were completely enfolded in the All That Is — God. We were formless, unchanging, immortal, and knew only love. Then, we had a thought. What would it be like, we wondered, if we were to descend into physical reality and experience the opposite energies — such as form, change, separation, fear, death, limitation, and duality? We played with the idea for a while, always thinking we could withdraw from the experiment any time we wished, should we indeed decide to put the thought into action. We saw no danger. Thus, the decision was made, and we lowered our energetic vibration to condense our energy into physical form. In the process, we forgot our connection to God and imagined we had actually separated from God and that we had no way back to the All That Is.

171

This dream became very real for us, and we then grew extremely guilt ridden for committing this *(original)* sin of separating from God. We became fearful that God would bring his wrath down upon us for having done so. This powerful belief in sin, guilt and fear became the Ego, and it became such a powerful force in our lives that it created in our minds a world dominated by fear. Our world is still one where fear, rather than love, is the driving force.

Though we tend to personify it, the Ego is not an entity in and of itself. Neither does it represent our personality. The Ego represents a set of deeply-held beliefs that keep us totally convinced of our separateness from God. The extreme power exerted by these subconscious beliefs through the dynamics of guilt, fear, repression, and projection create the appearance that the Ego *lives* in us. The Ego keeps us stuck in the World of Humanity and asleep (unconscious), dreaming that we have separated from God.

Assumption: **When we decided to experiment with physical incarnation, God gave us total free will to live this experiment in any way we chose and to find for ourselves the way home to the All That Is.**

Free will is honored at the highest level. Contrary to what the Ego would have us believe, God was not mad at us for playing with the idea of separation. God gives us anything we want, whatever we choose and makes no judgment about it. Whenever we ask for help, through prayer and Radical Forgiveness, the call is always answered.

Assumption: **Life is not a random event. It has purpose and provides for the unfoldment of a divine plan with opportunities to make choices and decisions in every moment.**

Seen from the World of Humanity, it might appear that we arrive on this planet by biological accident. Our only significance lies in the fact that our parents made love and started a chain of biological events called pregnancy and birth.

It also might appear as if the only way to master the life experience lies in learning a lot about how the world works and in developing skills that enable us to control as much as possible the seemingly random circumstances of our lives. The more mastery we achieve over the physical circumstances of our lives, the better our lives appear to become.

The opposite is true when viewed from the World of Divine Truth. From this perspective, our arrival on the planet represents a deliberate, planned and conscious choice. The plan includes the selection of the people who will serve as our parents.

Also, the seemingly haphazard events of our lives are attributed to the unfoldment of a Divine plan, decided upon in advance, and totally purposeful in terms of our spiritual growth. The more we surrender to this unfoldment without trying to control it, the more peaceful we become.

173

At first blush, this seems a fatalistic viewpoint. However, this is not just fate. In truth, the Divine plan allows for a great deal of creativity and flexibility and continues to honor the principle of free will. We continue to co-create with Spirit the circumstances of our lives, and without exception, to get precisely what we want. The extent to which we resist (judge) what we get, determines whether we experience life as painful or joyful.

Mastery of the life experience, then, relies on us entering life fully and trusting that we are taken care of totally and supported all the time no matter what. Radical Forgiveness moves us in that direction.

Assumption: **Physical reality is an illusion created by our five senses. Matter consists of interrelating energy fields vibrating at different frequencies.**

Most people have a difficult time coming to grips with the idea that our physical reality is an illusion created by our senses. Ken Carey confirms the difficulty we have grasping this concept. In his book, which was a channeled work, the souls *talking through him* made an interesting observation.* They said that when they got inside Carey's body and experienced all his senses, they were simply amazed. Only then did they understand why human beings felt the physical world was real. Our senses make the illusion so convincing that even these disincarnate souls appreciated why we would have great difficulty getting beyond it.

---

* Carey. K. "Starseed Transmissions" (Uni*Sun, 1982),

Indeed, it is difficult to remember that the physical world is simply an illusion. However, we are beginning to move in a direction that fosters that memory. Recently, scientists have begun talking about the human body in terms of a **mind/body continuum.** Such terminology gives us the sense that our bodies are, indeed, more than cells, molecules and atoms. Energy science tells us that, in reality, our bodies are *dense condensations of interrelating energy fields* and that, just like a hologram, all matter consists of energy vibrating in certain patterns. Holograms are those seemingly real, three-dimensional images created by laser beams. Quantum physicists have theorized that the entire universe is a hologram and everything in it, including each one of us, is a hologram as well.

Some energy fields vibrate at frequencies that enable them to be observed and measured. They can be given physical qualities like weight, volume, hardness, and fluidity. We give such energy patterns names like wood, steel, leather, or whisky. Everything physical simply represents energy vibrating at a rate we can *detect* with our five senses.

Yet, this concept seems strange to us. We have developed such faith in our five senses to detect the physical world around us that we have difficulty imagining that our bodies consist of more than just what we can see and feel. Yet, in a very real sense, the physical world is an illusion *created* by our senses.

Consider for a moment one of the metal beams holding up a building. It looks solid enough, and our sense of touch

175

and sight tell us that it is solid, as well as strong and heavy. However, we also know that this beam is composed entirely of atoms. Our knowledge of atoms tells us that each atom is composed of a nucleus of protons around which orbits at ultra high speed one or more electrons.

To get a feel for the spacial relationship between the nucleus and the electron, imagine a basketball sitting in the middle of a football stadium. Now imagine an object the size of a golf ball orbiting the basketball at several thousand miles per hour and describing a circle with a diameter as large as the stadium. This gives us a rough picture of the kind of size difference we are talking about between an electron and a nucleus and the immense space between them.

From this, we can say that an atom is composed of somewhere around 99.99% space. Since matter is composed entirely of atoms, matter must be composed of 99.99% space. Thus, the aforementioned metal beam is 99.99% space. *You* are 99.99% space as well.

The beam looks so dense for the same reason that an electric fan when running looks solid. When such a fan is not rotating you can see the spaces between the blades, and you can put your hand through those spaces. When the blades spin very fast, you can no longer see the spaces. In addition, if you try putting your hand between the blades, they feel like an impenetrable wall. Like a fan's blades, any piece of physical material is comprised of a mass of electrons spinning so fast that they appear solid to our senses.

If the electrons in the beam holding up the building were to stop spinning, the beam would disappear in an instant. If all the other electrons around it stopped spinning too, we could imagine the whole building disappearing. No debris would be left, no dust, nothing. To a viewer, it would appear that the building had simply evaporated or disappeared.

Matter is simply vibration — nothing more, nothing less. Our senses are tuned to these vibrations, and our minds convert them into matter. Sounds weird, but it's true.

Assumption: **We have subtle bodies as well as physical bodies. Our physical body vibrates at the frequency of matter (the World of Humanity), while the highest two of the five subtle bodies vibrate closer to the frequency of the Soul (the World of Divine Truth).**

Besides the flesh and bone of our physical bodies, we consist of other energy patterns we cannot see or measure. These are called our *subtle bodies* or *subtle fields*. They vibrate at frequencies an octave or two higher than those bodies condensed as matter and are beyond the range of our senses and most detection instrumentation. These are:

The Etheric Body
The etheric body carries the energetic template of the body. It ensures the continuation of the patterns, harmonies and disharmonies within the body while the body constantly renews itself. Your body is not the same as one year ago, for not one cell exists in your body that is more than one year old.

177

The etheric body interacts with your genetic code and holds the memory of who you are, the shape of your nose, your height, what prejudices you hold, what you like to eat, your strengths, your weakness, your illness patterns, etc.

The Emotional Body

The emotional body vibrates one octave above the etheric field. Also known as the astral body, it suffuses the etheric field and the bioenergetic fields of the physical body and manifests in the body as feelings.

An emotion constitutes a thought attached to a feeling that usually results in a physical response or action. When energy flows freely from the emotional field through the etheric field and the physical body, everything works together beautifully.

When we restrict our emotional energy through suppression or repression, we create energy blocks in both our etheric and emotional fields as well as in our physical body.

The perceptual shift required for forgiveness cannot happen while anger and resentment are maintained in the emotional body. Any energy stuck in the emotional body must be cleared first.

The Mental Body

This field governs our intellectual functioning and is responsible for memory, rational thinking, concrete thought, and so on. Of course, there are scientists who still maintain that thinking and other mental processing can be explained in terms of brain biochemistry. Suffice it to say that the scientists who follow the logic of quantum physics believe that the mind goes beyond the brain, beyond even the body. They believe that brain and mind interact *holographically* and that each cell contains a blueprint of the whole. Many researchers believe that memory resides in holographic form in an energetic field that exists beyond the body.

Proof of this is continually showing up as a by-product of organ replacement surgery. One celebrated story concerns a person who received a liver transplant. Some months after the operation, he began having a recurring dream that did not make sense to him. After some investigation, he discovered that the person who had donated the liver had dreamt the same dream for many years. The memory of that dream was apparently imbedded in the cellular structure of the liver.

The Causal Body or Intuitional Field

At the next octave up lies the body we might call our soul, Higher Self or our connection to the World of Divine Truth. Also called the causal body, this one provides our bridge to the spiritual realm. Whereas the mental field deals with ideas and thought forms at the concrete level, this field deals with them at the conceptual, abstract, iconic, and symbolic level. It deals with essence, intuition and *direct knowing*. The causal body extends beyond the individual and penetrates the *collective mind* — or what Jung called the *collective unconscious,* a single mind to which we all individually connect and find access.

179

The idea of subtle bodies rising in harmonics is by no means new; it has been included in many great spiritual traditions throughout the whole world, especially those of the East.

Assumption: **Universal energy as life force and consciousness is brought into our body via the chakra system. The first three chakras are aligned with the World of Humanity while the fourth through eighth align more closely with the World of Divine Truth.**

In addition to the ocean of energy containing our differently-vibrating subtle bodies, we human beings possess a system of energy centers that align vertically in our bodies. These are known as chakras — *wheels of energy* in Sanskrit, because they are like vortices of spinning energy.

The chakras act like transformers. They take the energy or life force (prana, chi, Christ energy) that comes to us from the universe and step it down to frequencies that can be used by the bio-molecular and cellular processes of the physical body. The chakras also represent the locations where each of the subtle bodies link to the physical body, thus bringing different levels of consciousness into our being. They process our daily experiences, thoughts and feelings while also carrying long-term data relating to personal and tribal history, long-established thought patterns and archetypes.

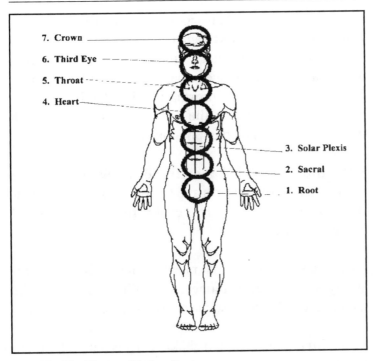

Fig. 13: The Human Chakra System.

The first three chakras possess levels of consciousness vibrating at the lower frequencies of the existential chain and rooted in the World of Humanity. They carry the energy of the victim archetype. Traditional forgiveness is the only type of forgiveness possible with the consciousness of the first three chakras. The consciousness that comes through the fifth, six, seventh, and eighth chakras are more likely to align with energies from the World of Divine Truth, while the fourth, the heart chakra, provides the link between the World of Humanity and the World of Divine Truth.

In addition, each chakra is associated with an endocrine gland and corresponds to a particular nerve nexus in the same area. Each also has a color and sound associated with it, and each nourishes a particular part of the body. Chakras also serve as information data-banks and processors associated with the parts of the body to which they are attached and the functions they serve.

• The **first** (root) chakra carries data relating to being grounded to Mother Earth and issues of basic trust, security and the will to live. This chakra runs on tribal/social consciousness.

• The **second** (sacral) chakra carries data relating to creativity, sexual energy, money, and guilt. This chakra, like the first, runs on tribal/social consciousness.

• The **third** (solar plexus) chakra carries data relating to power and control, social and familial relationships, betrayal, and anger. This chakra also is directed by tribal/social consciousness.

• The **fourth** (heart) chakra carries data about matters of the heart, relationships, love, nurturing, and compassion. This is the first chakra to energize individuality and self-determination independent of social group consciousness.

• The **fifth** chakra (throat) carries data about things expressed or withheld in matters of personal power, individual will and creative expression. It is directed by individual, as opposed to group, consciousness.

• The **sixth** (3rd eye) chakra carries data relative to intuitive knowledge, clairvoyance and the will to know the truth. In this case, truth refers to knowing not defined by group consciousness, but directly from individual experience of cosmic consciousnes.

• The **seventh** (crown) chakra carries data about spiritual awareness and connection to Source.

• The **eighth** chakra, which lies above the head, represents our contract or agreement for incarnation and contains our life's mission.

Though central to eastern medical traditions, the chakra system gets zero attention from western medical science and there exists very little recognition generally in the west of its central importance to our health, spiritual well-being and vibratory rate.

In truth, they are crucial. When these energy centers become out of balance — as they do when we become emotionally upset or traumatized for instance — they reverse rotation, become very erratic and in some cases close down almost entirely. Anger, resentment and hurt will tend to close the heart chakra and the throat chakra, guilt and lack of trust will weaken the sacral chakra, and so on. The effects of such energy imbalances will be felt as lethargy, a general malaise, low sex drive, inability to speak our truth and a whole host of symptoms for which a medical cause cannot be found. If the chakras remain out of balance for a long time however, it is inevitable that an effect will indeed, sooner or later, manifest as disease in the physical body. As we noted with the subtle bodies, disease almost always begins in the energy fields — which include the chakras — and moves into the physical body appearing finally as disease or physical breakdown.

Fortunately, chakras can be restored to balance quite easily. There are practitioners who are sensitive enough to feel the energy of each chakra and have techniques for rebalancing them. Most forms of energy medicine such as acupuncture, homeopathy, aromatherapy and many others act directly on the chakras and bring them into balance.

(For a thorough explanation of how our evolution can be explained by reference to the chakras, see "Anatomy of the Spirit," by Caroline Myss, (Three Rivers Press, 1996.)

PART FOUR

Tools for Radical Forgiveness

16: A Spiritual Technology

In writing the first edition of this book I had two objectives in mind. First, I wanted to explain the concept of Radical Forgiveness as simply as I could to make it accessible to as many people as possible. Second, I wanted to make it as practical as I could so that people could use it in their everyday lives. That meant having tools that were not only effective but quick and easy to use.

As I write this second edition, I confess that the extent to which the tools in this book have proven effective more than surprises me. I find myself in awe of how extraordinarily powerful they have proven to be in helping people heal their lives.

I have also come to realize that they work in a way not dissimilar to how homeopathic remedies work. That is to say they work holo-energetically *(using the energy of the whole).*

Being part of a holographic universe, each minute part of the universe is not only connected energetically to the whole, but contains the whole. Therefore, from an energetic standpoint, you cannot change one part of it without it affecting the whole.

Homeopathy uses this principle by making remedies that effect the energy system of the organism in exactly this way. The tiniest part of an active ingredient is put into water and it is then diluted many thousands of times to the point where there is no physical trace of the substance left. What does remain however, is the energetic imprint of the substance and in that lies the power to heal. When the person takes the remedy, the subtle body registers the imprint and becomes stimulated to move energy in whatever way it needs in order to heal at all levels.

The same thing happens with these Radical Forgiveness tools. Just as someone might look at the homeopathic remedy and would, seeing only water, find great difficulty in imagining that it has the power to heal, so might someone looking at a forgiveness worksheet, for example, be totally sceptical about its ability to change their life.

Yet it works. Thousands of people have used the worksheet or listened to the 13 Steps CD, or walked the circle in the Radical Forgiveness Ceremony, and have experienced miracles in their lives.

These tools work because each of them is simply the delivery system for the secret ingredient — the energetic imprint of Radical Forgiveness; i.e. the *willingness* to be open to the idea that there is nothing to forgive.

The process is very subtle. Mind control or making things happen at the gross level through affirmations, visualization techniques or hypnosis has little relevance to Radical Forgiveness. Neither does it require a high level of belief or faith; nor do you need to be in a meditative or altered state. All you need to do is use a simple tool that asks little of you in the way of intelligence, discipline or skill. It asks only that you express a tiny amount of willingness—that's all. In this second edition of the book, I have even simplified the worksheet so that in some places you only have to check boxes in answer to a few questions. It still works.

Since forgiveness is always a 'fake-it-'til you-make-it,' proposition, we are indeed fortunate that it needs only that small amount. If you had to wait until you had 100% willingness to believe that the situation was perfect, you would never begin the process.

The following story is an example of how this transformation can occur in an instant using one of the Radical Forgiveness tools - interestingly enough, the quickest and simplest of them all — the *13 Steps to Radical Forgiveness.*

Debi and the 13 Steps

Debi was a studio singer which means she sang jingles, commercials, radio ID's and things like that. She was considered to be among the best in the business. In 1999, she came to study with me to become a Radical Forgiveness Coach.

At one point during the training, I wanted to teach her how to facilitate the *13 Steps to Radical Forgiveness.* It takes no more than seven minutes and involves responding in the affirmative to thirteen very simple questions.

The thirteen questions all relate to one's willingness (the secret ingredient) to see the perfection in the situation whether they understand it or not. The answer to each question is 'Yes.'

189

I asked Debi if she had a situation to work with for this process. She thought for a while and then said: *"Yes, here's something I've been upset about for a while. I'd almost forgotten. About thirteen years ago, I was in a particular studio and in came a guy that I knew reasonably well, but was not real close to. We chatted for a while and eventually he came out with what was really on his mind. He said, "Debi, I have this great product that's just perfect to market on the radio and I need you to do an ad for me. The problem is, I don't have money right now, but will you do it as a big favor to me?"*

Well, I finally gave in and agreed to do for $75 what I normally charge a lot of money for. I did the ad, and what d'you know, it made him a multi-millionaire overnight.

Sometime later, when I ran into him, I suggested he might want to send just a little bit of that my way in appreciation of what I had done for him. His response was, "Debi, we're not in the business of giving money away!"

This was perfect. She was obviously into her feelings about it —even after thirteen years! This was understandable given the fact that every time she had turned the radio on over the last thirteen years, there would be that ad! As you might imagine it had all the ingredients of a victim story—betrayal, insult, manipulation, withholding, ingratitude and so on.

So I immediately proceeded to take her through the process. It took no more than the seven minutes, and as always after doing a process like that, we went on to something else without any further discussion. (Talking about it would destroy the energy field created in the process).

She went out that evening and returned to her hotel at around 11:00 pm. She called me at 11:05 in a state of great excitement. Apparently she had checked her voice mail messages and one was from the studio producer who had helped her do that particular ad.

The message went like this: "Debi, that commercial you recorded for Mr. X., has come up again and it needs to be re-recorded. However, the copyright has expired so you could earn all the royalties on it this time. Are you interested?"

Well, as you might imagine, I was jumping up and down yelling, "Hey, this stuff really works!" But then Debi says, "But there's more. When we did the 13 steps," Debi went on, "I happened to glance at the clock on the wall, and for some reason I registered the time quite clearly in my mind. It was 3:01 pm. That message came in at 3:02 pm! One minute after— and I haven't spoken with him for months!"

Debi's victim story about how she was 'used,' cheated, dishonored, insulted and rejected had kept the energy stuck for thirteen years. It was not until she was invited to express a minute amount of willingness to see that she had created that story out of her own perception of the situation, and during the 13 Steps process, reframed it in a way that reflected spiritual truth, that the energy field collapsed. At no point did we 'work' on her story. That would only have given it more power and reinforced it. Instead we used the holo-energetic technology of Radical Forgiveness to transform the energy.

191

It is interesting to look at what might have been happening here. Most people would have agreed with Debi that this man had betrayed, insulted and dishonored her by his selfish attitude. Yet the very fact that he exhibited this really quite peculiar kind of behavior was a clue that something else was going on beneath the apparent situation.

At the time that event occurred, Debi's self esteem was very low. Even though she was always being told how good a singer she was, she could never accept it. She would always put herself down. She had an unconscious belief that she wasn't worthy of what she could rightly charge for her talent.

It is a principle of Radical Forgiveness that if you have a limiting belief that prevents you from becoming whole or from achieving your true purpose, your Higher Self will always find a way to acquaint you with your limiting belief so you can heal it. It can't intervene directly because you have free will. But it can, through the Law of Attraction, bring into your life someone who will act out your belief for you so you might see it for what it is and choose to let it go.

This man resonated with her limiting belief that she was unworthy, not good enough and undeserving and responded to the call. His Higher Self colluded with her Higher Self to play this worthiness issue out so she got to feel the pain of this idea in order that she might see it and choose again.

Far from being a villain then, this man was, in fact, a healing angel for Debi. At great discomfort to himself — for who would enjoy being a mean spirited jerk — he played out Debi's story for her. Unfortunately, she missed the lesson at that time and simply took it as an opportunity to enlarge her 'not-good-enough' story and to prove it right.

It is not until thirteen years later that she did a simple little process called *The 13 Steps.* As a result of that she gets to see the truth — that he was providing a healing opportunity for her and that he was in fact her *healer.* Immediately the energy starts to move again and the money flows almost instantly in her direction. (Money is just energy in another form.)

A few days after Debi returned from the training, she ran into him. He made a point of coming up to her and saying, *"You know Debi, I never did thank you for what you did for me all those years ago when you did that first ad for me. You gave me a break and it worked. I really appreciate it. Thank you."* He still didn't offer her money but that doesn't matter. What she got from him was the acknowledgment that she was previously unable to accept. That was the final healing moment.

Since then, Debi has stepped out into her power. She quit hiding her talent doing anonymous studio work and is now out there doing concerts and recording her own CDs. She has even started her own production company. All that old 'I'm not good enough' stuff has disappeared completely and she is living her purpose.

If and when you purchase the Companion CD advertised on the inside back cover of this book, listen to Debi singing "Beyond Justice to Mercy," on track number two. You'll hear what I mean!

I always tell Debi's story to convince people of the power of these seemingly simple tools and to encourage people to use them and I am grateful to her for allowing me to do so.

Note:

If you would like to experience the power of the 13 Steps to Forgiveness and own a tool that will continually help you live this ideal, send for the Companion CD. (See inside back cover.)

I have recorded on the CD an Introduction to the 13 Steps but it is on a separate track. That way, you don't have to listen to it every time you do the 13 Steps, but you will find it helpful. The process itself only takes about five minutes. The ideal place to keep the CD is in the car. Any time something upsets you, pop it in and listen.

For no other reason than because it has the 13 Steps on it, this CD is probably the best investment that you will ever make in yourself.

17: The Five Stages of RF

No matter the form that the technology of Radical Forgiveness takes, whether it be a workshop, the 13 Steps, the Radical Forgiveness worksheet or the ceremony, each is designed to take you through the five essential stages of Radical Forgiveness. These are:

1. Telling the Story:

In this step, someone willingly and compassionately listens to us tell our story, and honors it as being our truth in the moment. (If we are doing a worksheet, this person might be ourself).

Having our story heard and witnessed is the first and vital step to letting it go. Just as the first step in releasing victimhood is to own it fully, so must we own our story in its fullness from the point of view of being a victim and avoid any spiritual interpretation at this stage. This comes later in step 4.

Here, we must begin from where we are (or were, if we are going back into the past to heal something), so that we can feel some of the pain that caused the energy block in the first place.

2. Feeling the Feelings:

This is the vital step that many so-called spiritual people want to leave out thinking that they shouldn't have 'negative' feelings. That's denial, pure and simple, and misses the crucial point that authentic power resides in our capacity to feel our feelings fully and in that way show up as fully human. It is only when we give ourselves permission to access our pain that our healing begins. The healing journey is essentially an emotional journey. But it doesn't have to be all pain either. It is surprising as we go down through the levels of emotion and allow ourselves to feel the authentic pain, how quickly it can turn to peace, joy and thankfulness.

3. Collapsing the Story:

This step looks at how our story began and how our interpretations of events led to certain (false) beliefs forming in our minds that have determined how we think about ourselves and how we have lived our lives. When we come to see that these stories are for the most part untrue and serve only to keep us stuck in the victim archetype, we become empowered to make the choice to stop giving them our vital life force energy. Once we decide to retrieve our energy, we take back our power and the stories wither and die.

It is also at this step that we might exercise a high degree of compassion for the person we are forgiving and bring to the table some straightforward honest to goodness understanding of how life often is, just how imperfect we all are and the realization that we are all doing the very best we can with what we are given. Much of this we might categorize as traditional forgiveness but it is nevertheless important as a first step and a reality check. After all, most of our stories have their genesis in early childhood when we imagined that the whole world revolved around us and that everything was our fault.

So this is where we can give up some of that child-centered woundedness merely by bringing our adult perspective to bear on it and confronting our own inner child with the plain truth of what really did or didn't happen as distinct from our interpretations about what we think happened. It is amazing how ridiculous many of our stories seem once we allow the light in. However, the real value in this step is in our releasing our attachment to the story so we can more easily begin to make the transition required in the next step.

4. Reframing the Story:

This is where we allow ourselves to shift our perception in such a way that instead of seeing the situation as a tragedy, we become willing to see that it was in fact exactly what we wanted to experience and was absolutely essential to our growth. In that sense it was perfect. At times we will be able to see the perfection right away and learn the lesson immediately. Most often however, it is a matter of giving up the need to figure it out and surrendering to the idea that the gift is contained in the situation whether we know it or not. It is in that act of surrender that the real lesson of love is learned and the gift received. This is also the step of transformation for as we begin to become open to seeing the Divine perfection in what happened, our victim stories that were once the vehicles

197

for anger, bitterness and resentment become transformed into stories of appreciation, gratitude and loving acceptance.

5. Integration:

After we have allowed ourselves to be willing to see the perfection in the situation and turned our stories into ones of gratitude, it is necessary to integrate that change at the cellular level. That means integrating it into the physical, mental, emotional and spiritual bodies so it becomes a part of who we are. It's like saving what you have done on the computer to the hard drive. Only then will it become permanent.

I find that 'Satori' breathwork is a very good way to integrate the change whether it is done as part of the workshop or soon thereafter. This entails lying down and breathing consciously in a circular fashion to loud music. (See Chapter 27).

With the worksheet, the integration comes through the writing and reading the statements out loud. With the 13 Steps it is making the verbal affirmation to see the perfection. With the ceremony it is in the act of walking across the circle and saying something of an affirmative nature to someone else coming in the other direction. Ritual, ceremony and, of course, music is also used to integrate the shift in perception that is Radical Forgiveness.

These five stages don't necessarily occur in this order. Very often we move through them, or some of them at least, simultaneously, or we keep coming back and forth from one stage to another in a kind of circular or spiralling fashion.

18: Fake It 'Til You Make It

Forgiveness is a journey and it begins always from a place of non-forgiveness. Getting there can take years or minutes and we know now that this is a matter of choice. Traditional forgiveness takes a long time, but we can do it quickly through Radical Forgiveness simply by expressing our *willingness* to see the perfection. Each time we do this, it represents an act of faith, a prayer, an offering, a humble request for Divine assistance. We do this at moments when we feel unable to forgive and in that sense it is a fake-it-'til-you-make it process.

Surrendering

Faking it until you make it really means surrendering to the process, putting forth no effort nor trying to control the results. In the Seattle study (Chapter 13), the more effort the participants put into trying to forgive, the more difficult they found it to let go of their hurt and anger. When they stopped trying to forgive and to control the process, at some point in time forgiveness just happened.

It is true that the energetic shift from anger and blame to forgiveness and responsibility happens much more quickly with Radical Forgiveness, because using the tools given here, we can drop the victim consciousness. Consciousness, you will recall from Chapter 13, changes time. Nevertheless, even with Radical Forgiveness we must enter the process with no expectation of when an energy shift might happen — even though we know that it can happen instantaneously. Exactly when the results begin to show up may depend on things we know little about. It might take a while before we begin to really feel unconditional acceptance for the person involved and peace around the situation — which is how we know when the forgiveness process is complete. It might take many worksheets, for example, to reach this point.

However, it will be of comfort to many to learn that we do not have to like the person to forgive them. Neither do we have to stay in their company if their personality and/or their behavior is toxic to us. Radical Forgiveness is a soul-to-soul interaction and requires only that we become connected at the soul level. When we feel this unconditional love for their soul, our soul joins theirs and we become one.

Taking the Opportunity

Any time someone upsets us, we must recognize this as an opportunity to forgive. The person upsetting us may be resonating something in us that we need to heal, in which case, he or she gives us a gift, if we choose to see it that way; that is, if we care to *shift our perception*. The situation also may be a replay of earlier times when someone did something similar to us. If so, this current person represents all the people who have ever done this to us before. As we forgive this person for the current situation, we forgive all others who behaved likewise, as well as forgiving ourselves for what we might have projected onto them.

An example of this appears as a diagram on page 36. Here, Jill's story is represented as a time-line on which appears all the opportunities she had been given to heal her original pain arising out of her misperception that she was 'not enough.' When she finally saw what was happening with the situation with Jeff and forgave him (healed), she automatically forgave and healed every previous occasion - including the original one with her father. Her entire story, including those connected to her previous husband, collapsed in an instant as soon as that light bulb went on.

This is why Radical Forgiveness requires no therapy as such. Not only does forgiving in the moment heal all the other times the same or similar thing happened, including the original situation, you don't even have to know what the original situation was. That means you don't have to go digging up the past trying to figure out exactly what the original pain was. It is healed anyway, so what's the point.

Shifting Our Perception

The following chapters contain processes that shift energy and offer opportunities to *change our perception* of what might be happening in a given situation. This change in perception constitutes the essence of Radical Forgiveness. All of these processes bring us into the present moment by helping us retrieve our energy from the past and withdraw it from the future, both of which must be done for change to occur. When we are in the present moment, we cannot feel resentment, because resentment only lives in the past. Neither can we feel fear, because fear only exists in relation to the future. We find ourselves, therefore, with the opportunity to be in present time and in the space of love, acceptance and Radical Forgiveness.

First Aid Forgiveness Tools

Some of the tools included in this section are more appropriate for use at the very moment when a situation requiring forgiveness occurs. They help jerk us into an awareness of what may be happening before we get drawn too deeply into a drama and go to victimland. When our *buttons get pushed,* we easily move straight into the defense/attack cycle. Once in this cycle, however, we find it tough to get out. Use of these quick tools, however, helps us avoid ever beginning the cycle. The Four-Steps to Forgiveness process is one of these. It is easy to remember and you can say it to yourself in the moment. The 13 Steps to Forgiveness tape or CD is also very useful because you can have that in the car or handy at home.

Other tools described in the following chapters are designed for use in quiet solitude after we have had a chance to vent anger and frustration. The Radical Forgiveness Worksheet works wonders in this regard. Use them all as an act of faith in the beginning. The payoff will prove incredible in time. Consistent use of these tools helps us find a peace we may never have known was even possible.

19: Feeling the Pain

Feeling the feelings is the second stage in the forgiveness process and usually arises as a consequence of telling the story. This step requires that we give ourselves permission to feel the feelings we have around a given situation — and to feel them fully. If we try to forgive using a purely mental process, thus denying that we feel angry, sad, or depressed, for example, nothing happens. I have met many people, especially those who think of themselves as spiritual, who feel that feelings are to be denied and 'given-over' to Spirit. That's what is known as a spiritual bypass.

In 1994, I agreed to do a workshop in England. This was ten years after I emigrated to America and I had quite forgotten the extent to which English people resist feeling their feelings.

The workshop was to take place in a monastery somewhere in the west of England, and as it happened most of the participants were spiritual healers.

We arrived at the monastery but there was no one around, so we went in, rearranged the furniture and began the workshop. I began by explaining that life was essentially an emotional experience for the purpose of our spiritual growth and that the workshop was designed to help us get in touch with emotions that we have buried. Well, you would have thought I was telling them that they had to dance naked around a fire or something! Here's what they said.

"Oh, no. We are spiritual. We have transcended our emotions. We don't give our emotions any credence at all. If we have them, we simply ask Spirit to take them away and we simply go straight to peace. We don't believe in this kind of work."

By about one hour into the workshop, I knew I had a disaster on my hands. It was like swimming through treacle. I couldn't get through at all, and there was no way they were going to do this work. I was feeling progressively more awful every moment and was convinced that the workshop was going to fall apart completely.

At this point Spirit intervened. A young monk in full habit burst into the room demanding to know who was in charge. When I said I was, he demanded that I go outside with him. He wanted to 'talk' to me, but I could see that he was seething with anger. He was all red and puffed up. I said that I was conducting a seminar and that I would come and find him when I was finished.

He went out very upset but came back almost immediately, clearly enraged. He pointed his finger at me and then hooked it as if to motion me towards him, and screamed. "I want to see you, right now!"

It was the gesture with the finger that got me. All the frustration and tension of the last hour came rushing to the surface. I turned to my class and said in a very menacing tone. *"Just watch this!"* I strode over to the red-faced puffed-up monk and told him in no uncertain tones, pointing back at him with my finger very close to his face, *"I don't care what you are wearing and what those clothes represent, you don't come into my workshop and hook me out as if I were some little schoolboy who has offended you. I'll come out and talk to you when — and only when — I am ready. In fact, I will be done right at 12:00 noon. If you have anything to say to me, you'd better be outside in the lobby right at that time. Then we can talk. Now, get out of my room!"*

I strode back to my class, all of whom were sitting there aghast, with their mouths gaping. (You don't talk to religious figures like that!) *"Right,"* I said, pointing to each one of them in turn, *"I want to know what you are feeling right now, in this moment, and don't give me that B.S. that you have given it to the violet flame and that you are feeling peaceful, because it is obvious that you are not. What are you feeling?!!! Get real!!"*

Well, needless to say they were in their feelings big time and we started to discuss them. With the help of the monk, I had broken through their wall of resistance to acknowledging that humans have feelings and that they are OK. I had busted their story. They were doing the spiritual bypass and I let them know it.

At 12:00 noon, I went out of the room into the lobby. The monk was there. I went straight up to him and, much to his surprise and consternation, I hugged him. *"Thank you so much,"* I said, *"You were a healing angel for me today. You were my seminar. You saved the whole thing."*

He really didn't know what to say. I don't think he got it either, even when I tried to explain it to him. He had calmed down though and it turned out that all he was so upset about was that I had not rung the bell to let him know that we were there. He had been sitting in his room waiting for the bell to ring, not thinking that we might push open the door and go on in. Can you imagine getting so enraged about such a small thing? Do you think he might have had an abandonment, or 'not-good-enough' issue running?

That 7-day retreat became one of the best workshops I have ever done. That's because they got real and authentic. I took them into their pain, some of which dated back to incidences that happened in the war which they had never shared before. They got to realize that the power to heal is in the feelings, not in talking or thinking; not in affirmations, nor even meditation if it includes shutting out feelings.

Another myth is that there are two kinds of feeling; positive and negative and that negative ones must be avoided. The truth is there is no such thing as a negative emotion. They only become *bad* and have a negative effect on us when they are suppressed, denied or unexpressed. Positive thinking is really just another form of denial.

We Want the Emotional Experience

As human beings, we are blessed with the capability to feel our emotions. In fact, some say the *only* reason we have chosen this human experience arises from the fact that this is the only planet carrying the vibration of emotional energy, and we have come here precisely to experience it. Consequently, when we do not allow ourselves to experience the full range of emotions and suppress them instead, our souls create situations in which we literally are forced to feel them. (Haven't you noticed that people often are given opportunities to feel intense emotions just after having prayed for spiritual growth?)

This means that the whole point of creating an upset may simply lie in our soul's desire to provide an opportunity for us to feel a suppressed emotion. That being the case, simply allowing ourselves to have the feeling might allow the energy to move through us and the so-called problem to disappear immediately.

However, not all situations are dissolved that easily. When we try coping with a deep-seated issue and a remembrance of what seems an unforgivable transgression, such as sexual abuse, rape or physical abuse, it takes more than just experiencing our emotions to get to the point where we feel unconditional love for that person. Feeling the emotion fully is just the first step in faking it until we make it and definitely cannot be bypassed.

I am not saying that the emotional work will not benefit from insight gained through a shift in perception that might have occurred before the emotions were felt and expressed. It certainly will. However, the converse does not hold true; the perceptual shift required for Radical Forgiveness will not happen if the underlying repressed feelings are not released first.

Invariably, when we feel the desire to forgive someone or something, we have at some time felt anger toward them or it. Anger actually exists as a secondary emotion. Beneath anger lies a primary emotional pain, such as hurt pride, shame, frustration, sadness, terror, or fear. Anger represents *energy in motion* emanating from the suppression of that pain. Not allowing one's anger to flow can be likened to trying to cap a volcano. One day it will blow!

Stage one and two in the Radical Forgiveness process asks us to get in touch with not only the anger, but the underlying emotion as well. This means feeling it — not talking about it, not analyzing it, not labeling it, but experiencing it!

Love Your Anger

All too often when people talk about *letting go* of anger or *releasing* anger, they really mean trying to get rid of it. They judge it as wrong and undesirable — even frightening. They do not want to feel it so they just talk about it and try to process it intellectually, but that does not work. Trying to process emotion through talking about it is just another way to resist feeling it. That's why most talk therapies don't work. **What you resist persists**. Since anger represents energy in motion, resisting it just keeps it stuck within us — until the volcano erupts. Releasing anger actually means freeing the stuck energy of held emotions by allowing them to move freely through the body as feeling.

Doing some kind of *anger work* helps us experience this emotion purposely and with control.

Anger Work Moves Energy

What we call anger work is not really about anger. It is simply the process of getting energy stuck in the body moving again. It might be more appropriately called energy release work. Whatever we call it, the process can be as simple as screaming into a cushion (so as not to alarm neighbors), yelling in the car, beating cushions, chopping wood, or doing some other explosive physical activity.

Combining physical activity with the use of the voice seems to provide the key to successful energy release work. All too often we block the energy of emotion in the throat, whether that be anger, sadness, guilt or whatever else, so vocal expression should always be a part of the process. We should go into it, not with the idea of trying to rid ourselves of the feeling, but with the intention of feeling the intensity of it moving through our body—without thought or judgment. If we truly can surrender to the emotions, we will feel more alive than we have felt in a long while, and we will find that the energy has dissipated.

If Anger Is Scary

For many of us, the thought of bringing up anger may be too scary even to contemplate, especially if terror lies underneath the anger. The person who did these terrible things to us may still exert a strong influence on our subconscious mind. Under these circumstances, it would not be advisable to do anger work alone. Instead, we should work with someone who knows how to support us while we feel both the anger and the terror — someone with whom we feel safe and who has experience in helping people move through intense emotion. A counselor or psychotherapist of some kind would be a good choice. I also recommend doing Satori Breathwork (see Chapter 27), with a skilled practitioner. This provides a way to release emotion.

Anger Addiction Warning

A note of caution needs to be sounded here. It becomes all too easy to get addicted to anger. Anger feeds on itself and easily becomes resentment. Resentment relishes going over and over an old hurt, constantly revisiting the pain associated with it and venting the resultant anger in some form. It becomes a powerful addiction in and of itself.

We must realize that anger that persists serves no useful purpose. Consequently, once the energy of anger has been allowed to flow as feeling, we should use the energy to create a positive outcome. Maybe we need to set a boundary or a condition on future interactions with the person around whom our anger revolves. Perhaps we can make a decision of some kind, such as to be willing to feel compassion for the person or to forgive the person. Only when used as the catalyst for positive change, self-empowerment or forgiveness will we prevent the anger from becoming an addictive cycle.

20: Making Room for the Miracle

T he Radical Forgiveness worksheet has literally
changed thousands of people's lives. It is not easy
to explain how and why it accomplishes such dramatic results except to say that it helps people shift their
energy. In fact, you could say that doing the worksheet is,
in and of itself, an energy experience. It is analogous to
that provided by the homeopathic remedy, except here the
secret ingredient is the willingness to forgive - even when
you don't feel like it. The worksheet is simply a way of
expressing this willingness. That seems to release the stuck
energy in the situation which then seems to resolve itself
automatically.

Now that you have read the book you will understand that,
any time anyone upsets you or triggers negative emotion,
its your *opportunity to heal.* Where before you would
have been sucked into the drama, now you can reach for a
worksheet and start the forgiveness process.

Keep doing worksheets until the energy around the situation, person or incident dissipates. This could take days
or months. On the other hand, maybe just one worksheet
will produce the desired result. It all depends on what is
being resonated and the emotion being triggered.

Making Room for The Miracle

A Radical Forgiveness Worksheet

Date:_____ Worksheet #_____ **Subject: (X)** *Whomever you are upset about:* _____

1. The situation causing my discomfort, as I perceive it now, is:

2) **CONFRONTING X:** I am upset with you because:

2b) Because of what you did (are doing), **I FEEL:** *(Idendity your real emotions here).*

SPACE FOR ADDITIONAL COMMENTS

3. I lovingly recognize and accept my feelings, and judge them no more:	Willing:	Open:	Skeptical:	Unwilling:
4. I own my feelings. No-one can make me feel anything. My feelings are a reflection of how I see the situation:	Willing:	Open:	Skeptical:	Unwilling:
5. Even though I don't know why or how, I now see that my soul has created this situation in order that I learn and grow.	Willing:	Open:	Skeptical:	Unwilling:

6. I am noticing some clues about my life, such as repeating patterns and other features of my life that indicate that I have had many such healing opportunitiesin the past but I didn't recognize them as such at the time. *For example:*

7. I am willing to see that my mission or 'soul contract' included having experiences like this - for whatever reason.	Willing:	Open:	Skeptical:	Unwilling:

8. My discomfort was my signal that I was witholding love from myself and (X) by judging, holding expectations, wanting (X) to change and seeing (X) as less than perfect. *(List the judgments, expectations and behaviors that indicate you were wanting (X) to change)*

SPACE FOR ADDITIONAL COMMENTS

9. I now realize that I get upset only when someone resonates in me those parts of me I have disowned, denied, repressed and then projected onto them.	Willing:	Open:	Skeptical:	Unwilling::
10. (X)_____ is reflecting what I need to love and accept in myself.	Willing:	Open:	Skeptical:	Unwilling:
11. (X)_____ is reflecting a misperception of mine. In forgiving (X), I heal myself and recreate my reality.	Willing:	Open:	Skeptical:	Unwilling:
12. I now realize that nothing (X), or anyone else, has done is either right or wrong. I drop all judgment.	Willing:	Open:	Skeptical:	Unwilling:
13. I release the need to blame and to be right and I am **WILLING** to see the perfection in the situation just the way it is.	Willing:	Open:	Skeptical:	Unwilling:

14. Even though I may not know what, why or how, I now realize that you and I have both been receiving exactly what we each had subconsciously chosen and were doing a healing dance with and for each other.

Willing:	Open:	Skeptical:	Unwilling:

15. I bless you (X)_____ for being willing to play a part in my healing and honor myself for being willing to play a part in your healing.

Willing:	Open:	Skeptical:	Unwilling:

16. I release from my consciousness all feelings of: *(as in Box # 2b)*

17. I appreciate your willingness (x)_____ to mirror my misperceptions, and I bless you for providing me with the opportunity to practice Radical Forgiveness and Self Acceptance.

Willing:	Open:	Skeptical:	Unwilling:

4. REFRAMING THE STORY

18. I now realize that what I was experiencing (my victim story) was a precise reflection of my unhealed perception of the situation. I now understand that I can change this 'reality' by simply being willing to see the perfection in the situation. For example........ *(Attempt a Radical Forgiveness re-frame which may simply be a general statement indicating that you just know everything is perfect, or specific to your situation if you can actually see what the gift is. Note: Often you cannot:)*

19. I completely forgive myself, _____ and accept myself as a loving, generous and creative being. I release all need to hold onto emotions and ideas of lack and limitation connected to the past. I withdraw my energy from the past and release all barriers against the love and abundance that I know I have in this moment. I create my life and I am empowered to be myself again, to unconditionally love and support myself, just the way I am, in all my power and magnificence.

20. I now SURRENDER to the Higher Power I think of as _____ and trust in the knowledge that this situation will continue to unfold perfectly and in accordance with Divine guidance and spiritual law. I acknowledge my Oneness and feel myself totally reconnected with my Source. I am restored to my true nature, which is LOVE, and I now restore love to (X) I close my eyes in order to feel the LOVE that flows in my life and to feel the joy that comes when the love is felt and expressed.

5. INTEGRATING THE SHIFT

21. A Note To You (X) _____ Having done this worksheet, I.........

I completely forgive you (x)_____ for I now realize that you did nothing wrong and that everything is in Divine order. I acknowledge, accept and love you unconditionally just the way you are. *(Note: This doesn't mean that you condone the behavior or you can't state a boundary.. That's World of Humanity stuff anyway)*

22. A Note To Myself:

I recognize that I am a spiritual being having a human experience, and I love and support myself in every aspect of my humanness.

Taken from the book "Radical Forgiveness" By Colin Tipping. **Acknowledgements:** Dr. Michael Ryce, Arnold M. Patent.
© 2001 Colin Tipping: Not for re-publication but please photocopy and share with others.
For further information or master copies of the worksheet, go to *www.radicalforgiveness.com*

The worksheet given on the previous two pages can be enlarged and photocopied, but you might prefer to download a full-size one from our web site. (See next page).

Completing the worksheet requires a reasonable grasp of the principles underlying Radical Forgiveness and the following *notes* serve as a reminder of them. The relevant parts of the worksheet are highlighted and by way of example, *filled in* as *if Jill had completed it at the time she was going through the situation with Jeff as portrayed in Jill's Story, Part 1.*

When we start with Radical Forgiveness, we have a tendency to want to do too many worksheets on too many people from our list, and to work immediately with the major issues of the past.

However, one of Radical Forgiveness' best characteristics lies in the fact that we do not have to dig up the past to heal it. Whomever is upsetting you *right now* is the person who represents ALL the people who have ever upset you for the same reason in the past. So work with that person first, even if you're thinking that it's no big deal. If it's upsetting you, it *is* a big deal. It could easily lead you to what really matters.

You might want to start with the smaller issues; ones that are fairly simple and without a great deal of emotional charge. Small problems grow into big ones if they are not dealt with, so you will be doing important work even with seemingly trivial situations. Besides that, it is much easier to learn how to create the necessary shifts in perception

215

with simpler, less traumatic situations. Leave the big ones for later.

You might want to date and number these sheets and then file them. This allows you to review them from time to time and to evaluate the extent to which your consciousness has changed. Alternatively, you might want to do a ritual burning of them as part of the process.

Special Acknowledgments

This worksheet has its origins in one created some years ago by Dr. Michael Ryce, a pioneer in this field who has dedicated his life to bringing the message of forgiveness to everyone on the planet, and in the work of Arnold M. Patent. Arnold originally introduced me to spiritual principle and his work inspires many of the steps in this forgiveness worksheet. I am deeply grateful for the contributions each have made to my understanding and, by extension, to this book.

Download a **FREE** Worksheet:

Go to our web site, www.radicalforgiveness.com, click on 'Worksheet Tutorial,' and download a full-size worksheet. You will have to register first, so while you're there, you might want to try the on-line interactive worksheet. (See page 294). People seem to love it and even prefer it to the paper one. See what you think. Alternatively, you can purchase a plastic laminated worksheet from the web site or by calling 1-888-755-5696.

Making Room For The Miracle
A Radical Forgiveness Worksheet

Date: *8/7/91*   Worksheet #   *3*

Subject (X) Whomever or whatever you are upset about   *JEFF*

• Identify the person, situation or object about which you feel upset, here noted as "X." In certain circumstances it may be yourself, but there is a big trap in doing this, especially when you first start doing this work. The trap is that because guilt is at the root of all separation, we are much too inclined to beat ourselves up at every opportunity. In my workshops, I tell people not to do it for that reason. All forgiveness is self forgiveness in the end, but it is best achieved in my opinion by forgiving and extending love outwards to others. It is universal law that it is always returned and you discover yourself as having been forgiven.

Be sure to write about him/her/it/yourself in the third person context. In other words, tell your story as if you were telling someone what happened or is happening. Use names.

---

1. The situation causing my discomfort, as I perceive it now, is:

Jeff is abandoning me by focussing all his attention and love on his daughter Lorraine -- completely ignoring me. He makes me wrong and accuses me of being mentally unbalanced. He makes me feel worthless and stupid. Our marriage is over and its all his fault. He is forcing me to leave him.

---

1. This section asks you to tell the story about your upset. Define the situation. Do not hold back. Describe how it feels for you right now. Do not edit or overlay it with any spiritual or psychological interpretation. You must honor where you are now, even if you know that you are in the World of Humanity, Ego and illusion. Knowing that you are experiencing illusion, and that you need to experience it, represents the first step toward escaping from it.

Even if we have raised our vibration considerably and spend a fair bit of our lives in the World of Divine Truth, we can easily be knocked off balance and find ourselves back in the world of Ego seeing ourselves as victims and all that goes with that. Being human requires that experience. We cannot always be joyful and peaceful and see the perfection in absolutely every situation.

---

2 (a) CONFRONTING X: I am upset with you because:

You have ruined our marriage. You have hurt me and rejected me. Your behavior stinks and I am going to leave you, you bastard!

2a. Be as confrontive as possible with X, and lay out exactly what you blame him/her/it for. This section's small space only allows a few words, but let the words you choose represent the totality of your upset. If the object or situation has no name, give it one, or at least write about it as if it were a person. If the person is dead, speak to him or her as if he or she were there in front of you. If you want to write it out in full, do so in the form of a letter. (See Chapter 24.) This step allows you to address the person directly. However, keep to one issue. Do not discuss other things in the letter, or on this worksheet. Reaching your objective— Radical Forgiveness—requires you to get clarity on precisely what you feel so upset about *now*.

---

2 (b) Because of what you did (are doing), I feel: *(Identfy your real emotions here)*

Deeply hurt, abandoned, betrayed. I feel very alone and sad. You've made me angry.

2b. It is vitally important that you allow yourself to feel your feelings. Do not censor them or *stuff* them. Remember, we came into the physical realm to experience emotion—the essence of being human. All emotions are good, except when we suppress them. Stuffing emotion creates potentially harmful energy blocks in our bodies.

Make sure the emotions you identify represent real emotions that you actually feel, not just *thoughts* about how you feel. Are you *mad, glad, sad,* or *afraid?* If you cannot be specific, that is okay. Some people find themselves unable to differentiate one feeling from another. If that holds true for you, just notice what general emotional quality you can feel around the situation.

If you would like to feel your emotions more clearly or strongly, pick up a tennis racquet or a bat and beat the heck out of some cushions or pillows. Use something that will make a noise when you hit the cushions. If anger scares you, have someone with you when you do this exercise. That person should encourage and support you in feeling your anger (or any other emotion) and make it safe to do so. Screaming into a cushion also helps release feelings. As I have stressed many times, the more you allow yourself to feel the hurt, sadness or fear that might lie beneath your anger, the better.

	(Check the appropriate box),			
3. I lovingly recognize and accept my feelings, and judge them no more.	Willing	Open	Skeptical	Unwilling

3. This important step provides you with an opportunity to allow yourself some freedom from the belief that feelings like anger, vengefulness, jealousy, envy, even sadness are bad and should be denied. No matter what they are, you need to feel your emotions in exactly the way they occur for you, for they are an expression of your true self. Your soul wants you to feel them fully. Know they are perfect and quit judging yourself for having them.

Try the following three-step process for integrating and accepting your feelings:

1. Feel the feeling fully, and then identify it as either mad, glad, sad, or afraid.

2. Embrace the feelings in your heart just the way they are. *Love them. Accept them.* Love them as part of yourself. Let them be perfect. You cannot move into the joy vibration without first

accepting your feelings and making peace with them. Say this affirmation: *"I ask for support in feeling love for each of my emotions just the way it is, as I embrace it within my heart and accept it lovingly as part of myself."*

3. Now *feel love for yourself* for having these feelings and know you have chosen to feel them as a way of moving your energy towards healing.

4. I own my feelings. No one can make me feel anything. My feelings are a reflection of how I see the situation.

Willing	Open	Skeptical	Unwilling

4. This statement reminds us that no-one can make us feel anything. Our emotions are our own. As we feel, recognize, accept, and love them unconditionally as part of ourselves, we become entirely free to hold on to them or let them go. This realization empowers us by helping us realize that the problem resides not *out there* but *in here*, within ourselves. This realization also represents our first step away from the victim archetype vibration. When we think other people, or even situations, make us mad, glad, sad, or afraid, we give them all our power.

5. Even though I don't know why or how, I now see that my soul has created this situation in order that I learn and grow.

Willing	Open	Skeptical	Unwilling

5. This is probably the most important statement on the worksheet. It reinforces the notion that thoughts, feelings and beliefs create our experiences and that furthermore, we order our reality in such a way as to support our spiritual growth. When we open ourselves to this truth, the problem almost always disappears. That's because there are no problems, only misperceptions.

The statement challenges us to accept the possibility that the situation may be purposeful and to let go of the need to know the how and the why of it.

This is where most intellectually inclined people have the greatest difficulty. They want 'proof' before they believe anything. Therefore they make knowing 'why' a condition for accepting the situation as a healing opportunity.

This is a dead end trap since to ask how and why things happen as they do is to ask to know the mind of God. At the level we are now in our spiritual development we cannot possibly know the mind of God. We must therefore give up our need to know why (which is a victim's question anyway), and surrender to the idea that God does not make mistakes and therefore everything is in Divine order.

The importance of this step comes in its ability to help you feel your way out of the victim mode into the possibility that the person, object or situation with whom you have the issue reflects precisely that part of yourself that you have rejected and which cries out to be accepted. It acknowledges that the Divine essence within, the knowing part of yourself, your soul — whatever you want to call it, has set the situation up for you, so you can learn, grow and heal a misperception or a false belief.

This step also creates self-empowerment. Once we realize we have created a situation, we have the power to
change it. We can choose to see ourselves as the victim
of circumstance, or we can choose to see our circumstance
as an opportunity to learn and to grow and to have our
lives be the way we want.

Do not judge yourself for creating a situation. Remember, the Divine part of yourself created it. If you judge
the Divine part of you, you judge God. Acknowledge yourself as a wonderful, creative, Divine being with the ability
to create your own lessons along the spiritual path, lessons
that eventually will take you home. Once you are able to
do this, you are able to surrender to the Divine essence
that you are and to trust it to do the rest.

> **6.** I am noticing some clues about my life, such as repeating
> patterns and other 'coincidences' that indicate that I have had
> many such healing opportunities in the past but I didn't recognize
> them as such at the time. *For example:*

6. This step recognizes that we are curious human beings
and that we have an insatiable need to know why things
happen as they do. So having said above that we must
abandon our need to know, this step offers us the chance
to have some fun looking for some of the more obvious
clues that would offer us evidence that the situation always
was perfect in some unexplainable way. So long as we do
not make having such evidence a prerequisite for accepting that this was so, there is no harm in it and it may turn on
some light bulbs. Bear in mind too, that there may well be

nothing that strikes you as evidence one way or the other. If nothing stands out, don't worry. Just leave the box blank and go on to the next item on the worksheet. It does NOT mean that the statement is any less true.

The kind of clues to look out for might be as follows:

1. Repeating Patterns: This is the most obvious one. Marrying the same kind of person over and over again is an example. Picking life partners who are just like your mother or father is another. Having the same kind of event happening over and over is a clear signal. People doing the same kind of things to you, like letting you down, or never listening to you, is another clue that you have an issue to heal in that area.

2. Number Patterns: Not only do we do things repetitively, but often do so in ways that have a numerical significance. We may lose our job every two years, fail in relationships every nine years, always create relationships in threes, get sick at the same age as our parents, find the same number turning up in everything we do, and so on. It is very helpful to construct a timeline like the one I did for Jill (see page 36), except that you might fill in all the dates and note all intervals of time between certain events. You might well find a meaningful timewise correlation in what is happening.

3. Body Clues: Your body is giving you clues all the time. Are you always having problems on one side of your body, or in areas that correlate to particular chakras and the issues contained therein, for example? Books by Caroline Myss, Louise Hay and many others will help you find meaning in what is happening to your body and what the healing message is. In our work with cancer patients, for example, the cancer always turned out to be a loving invitation to change or to be willing to feel, and heal repressed emotional pain.

4. Coincidences and 'Oddities.' This is a rich field for clues. Anytime anything strikes you as odd, or out of character, not quite as you'd expect or way beyond chance probability, you know you are onto something. For example, not only was it odd that in Jill's story, both girls who were getting the love that Jill felt was denied her were called Lorraine, which is not a common name in England, they were also both blonde, blue-eyed and the first born of three. Jeff's behavior was also extremely uncharacteristic. Far from being cruel and insensitive, Jeff is an exceedingly kind, nurturing and sensitive man. I can't imagine Jeff being cruel to anyone or anything. His behavior towards Jill certainly struck me as odd in the extreme.

Where once we thought things happened by chance and were just coincidences we are now willing to think that it is Spirit making things happen synchronistically for our highest good. It is these synchronicities that lie imbedded in our stories and once we see them as such, we become free then to feel the truth in the statement that 'my soul has created this situation in order that I learn and grow.'

7. I am willing to see that my mission or 'soul contract' included having experiences like this — for whatever reason.

Willing	Open	Skeptical	Unwilling

7. This statement is simply there to remind us of one of the assumptions of Radical Forgiveness, that we come into this life experience with a mission or an agreement with Spirit to do certain things, be a certain way or transform certain energies. Whatever that mission was or is, we simply know that whatever experiences we are having are part and parcel of the role we came into play. Princess Diana's story is a great example of that. Please note that the last part of the statement absolves us from the need to know what the mission was.

8. My discomfort was my signal that I was withholding love from myself and (X) by judging, holding expectations, wanting (X) to change and seeing (X) as less than perfect. *(List the judgments, expectations and behaviors that indicate you were wanting (X) to change).*

I realize that my committment was to making Jeff wrong and blaming him for my discomfort - when really I was responsible for it all the time. I was judging him and making him responsible for my happiness and requiring him to be different from the way he was. I was not recognizing the truth — that I am loved by him.

8. When we feel disconnected from someone, we cannot love them. When we judge a person (or ourselves) and make them wrong, we withhold love. Even when we make them right, we are withholding love, because we make our love conditional upon their *rightness* continuing.

226

Any attempt to change someone involves a withdrawal of love, because wanting them to change implies that they are wrong (need to change) in some way. Furthermore, we may even do harm in encouraging them to change, for though we may act with the best intentions, we may interfere with their spiritual lesson, mission and advancement.

This is more subtle than we realize. For instance, if we send unsolicited healing energy to someone because they are sick, we are in effect making a judgment that they are not OK as they are and should not be sick. Who are we to make that decision? Being sick may be the very experience they need to have for their spiritual growth. Naturally if they request a healing, then it becomes a different matter entirely and you do all you can in response to their request. Nevertheless, you still see them as perfect.

So make a note in this box of all the ways in which you want the person you are forgiving to be different or in what respects you want them to change. What subtle judgments do you make about the person which indicates your inability to accept them just the way they are? What behavior do you exhibit that shows you to be in judgment of them? You may be quite surprised to find that your well intentioned desire for them to be different *'for their own benefit,'* was really just a judgment on your part.

If the truth be known, it is precisely your judgment that creates his or her resistance to changing. Once you let go of the judgment, they will probably change. Ironic isn't it?

9. I now realize that I get upset only when someone resonates in me those parts of me I have disowned, denied, repressed and projected onto them.

Willing	Open	Skeptical	Unwilling

10. (X) _____ is reflecting what I need to love and accept in myself

Willing	Open	Skeptical	Unwilling

9 & 10. These statements acknowledge that when we get upset with someone, they are invariably reflecting back to us the very parts of ourselves that we most despise and have projected onto them.

If we can open ourselves enough to be willing to accept that this person is offering us a chance to accept and love a part of ourselves that we have condemned and that he or she is a healing angel in that sense, the work will have been done.

And as we have said before, you don't have to like the person. Just recognize them as a mirror, thank their soul by doing this worksheet and move on.

Neither do we need to figure out what parts of ourselves are being mirrored. Usually it is far too complicated anyway. Let it go at that and don't be drawn into an analysis. It works best without it.

11. (X) _____ is reflecting a misperception of mine. In forgiving (X), I heal myself and recreate my reality.

Willing	Open	Skeptical	Unwilling

228

11. This statement reminds us that through our stories which are always full of misperceptions, we create our reality and our lives. We will always draw people to us who will mirror our misperceptions and offer us the opportunity to heal the error and move in the direction of truth.

	Willing	Open	Skeptical	Unwilling
12. I now realize that nothing (X) or anyone else has done is either right or wrong. I drop all judgment.				

12. This step goes against everything that we have ever been taught about being able to distinguish between right and wrong, good and evil. After all, the whole world gets divided up along those lines. Yes, we know that the World of Humanity is really just an illusion, but that doesn't alter the fact that the human experiences demand that we make these particular distinctions in our daily lives.

What helps us with this step is realizing that we are only affirming that there is no right or wrong, good or bad when seeing things from the spiritual big picture standpoint — from the perspective of the World of Divine Truth. From there we are able to get beyond the evidence of our senses and minds and see Divine purpose and meaning in everything. Once we are able to see that, then we can see that there is no right or wrong. It just is.

	Willing	Open	Skeptical	Unwilling
13. I release the need to blame and to be right and I am WILLING to see the perfection in the situation, just the way it is.				

229

13. This step confronts you with the perfection in the situation and tests your willingness to see this perfection. While it never will be easy to see the perfection or good in something such as child abuse, we can be *willing* to see the perfection in the situation, be *willing* to drop the judgment and be *willing to drop the need to be right.* While it may always be difficult to recognize that both the abuser and the abused somehow created their situation to learn a lesson at the soul level, and that their mission was to transform the situation on behalf of all abused people, we can nevertheless be *willing* to entertain this thought.

Obviously, the closer we are to a situation, the more difficult it becomes to see its perfection, but seeing the perfection does not always mean understanding it. We cannot know the reasons why things happen as they do; we must simply have faith that they are happening perfectly and for the highest good of all.

Observe your strong need to be right. We possess an enormous investment in being right and we learned at an early age to fight to be right, which usually means proving that someone else is wrong. We even measure our self worth by how often we are right, thus it is no wonder that we have such trouble accepting that something just *is* — that it is neither inherently right nor wrong. If you really cannot at this point drop your judgment about something that seems awful, just reconnect with your feelings (see step #3 above), move into them and admit to yourself that you cannot yet take this step. However, *be willing* to drop your judgment. Willingness always remains the key.

Willingness creates the energetic imprint of Radical Forgiveness. As the energy shifts, all else follows.

14. Even though I may not know why or
how, I now realize that you and I have
been receiving exactly what we each
had subconsciously chosen and were
doing a healing dance with and for each other.

Willing	Open	Skeptical	Unwilling

14. This statement serves as yet another reminder of how
we can instantly become aware of our subconscious beliefs if we look at what shows up in our lives. What we
have at any particular point in time truly *is what we want.*
We have, at the soul level, chosen our situations and experiences, and our choices are not wrong. And this is true for
all parties involved in the drama. Remember, there are no
villains or victims, just players. Each person in the situation
is getting exactly what they want. Everyone is engaged in
a healing dance.

15. I bless you (X) _____ for being willing
to play a part in my healing and honor myself
for being willing to play a part in yours.

Willing	Open	Skeptical	Unwilling

15. It is entirely appropriate to bless (X) for co-creating
the situation with you so you could become aware of the
beliefs that create your life. (X) deserves your gratitude
and blessings since this co-creation and subsequent awareness gives you the ability to know your beliefs, which in
turn, empowers you with the ability to let them go. When
you do so, you can make another choice immediately about
your beliefs and what you want to create in your life. (X) is
entitled to feel the same gratitude for the same reasons.

231

16. I release from my consciousness all feelings of: (as in box 2b)

Hurt, abandonment, betrayal, aloneness sadness and anger.

16. This enables you to affirm that you release the feelings that you had noted in Box 2. As long as these emotions and thoughts remain in your consciousness, they block your awareness of the misperception that is causing the upset. If you still feel strongly about the situation, you still have an investment in whatever the misperception is — your belief, interpretation, judgment, etc. Do not judge this fact or try to change your investment. Just notice it.

Your emotions about your situation may come back time and time again, and you can make that okay, too. Just be willing to feel them and then release them, at least for the moment, so the light of awareness can shine through you and allow you to see the misperception. Then, once again, you can choose to see the situation differently.

Releasing emotions and corresponding thoughts serves an important role in the forgiveness process. As long as those thoughts remain operative, they continue lending energy to our old belief systems, which created the reality we now are trying to transform. Affirming that we release both the feeling and the thoughts attached to them begins the healing process.

17. I appreciate your willingness
(X) __*Jeff*__ to mirror my
misperceptions and bless you for
providing me with the opportunity to
practice Radical Forgiveness and Self Acceptance.

Willing	Open	Skeptical	Unwilling

17. This is another opportunity to feel gratitude for (X) having been in your life and for being willing to do the healing dance with you.

> **18.** I now realize that what I was experiencing (my victim story) was a precise reflection of my unhealed perception of the situation. I now understand that I can change this 'reality' by simply being willing to see the perfection in the situation. For example........ *(Attempt a Radical Forgiveness reframe which may simply be a general statement indicating that you just know everything is perfect, or specific to your situation if you can actually see what the gift is. Note: Often you cannot:)*
>
> *I now see that Jeff was simply mirroring my false belief that I was unlovable and he was giving me the gift of healing. Jeff loves me so much, he was willing to endure the discomfort of acting it out for me. I now see that I was getting everything I wanted for my own healing and that Jeff was getting what he wanted for his healing. The situation was perfect in that sense and is evidence of Spirit working in my life and that I am loved.*

18. If you are not able to see a new interpretation which is specific to your situation, that's not a problem. The Radical Forgiveness reframe might simply be expressed in a very general way, such as, "*what happened was simply the unfoldment of a Divine plan and that it was called forth by my own Higher Self for my spiritual growth* *and that the people involved were doing a healing dance with me so, in truth, nothing wrong ever happened."* Writing something like that would be perfectly adequate. On the other hand, if you did have some insights into how it all worked out in a perfect sense, that would be fine too.

What would NOT be helpful would be to write an interpretation based on assumptions rooted in the World of Humanity, like giving reasons why it happened or making excuses. You might be exchanging one BS story for another or even shifting into pseudo forgiveness. A new interpretation of your situation should allow you to feel its perfection from the spiritual standpoint, and become open to the gift it offers you. Your reframe should offer a way of looking at your situation that reveals the hand of God or Divine Intelligence working for you and showing you how much It loves you.

Note: *It may take completing many worksheets on the same issue to feel the perfection. Be absolutely truthful with yourself, and always work from your feelings. There are no right answers, no goals, no grades, and no end products here. The value lies in the process, in doing the work. Let whatever comes be perfect, and resist the urge to edit and evaluate what you write. You cannot do it wrong.*

> **19.** I completely forgive myself ___*Jill*___ and accept myself as a loving, generous, creative being. I release all need to hold onto negative emotions and ideas of lack and limitations. I withdraw my energy from the past and release all barriers against the love and abundance that I know I have already. I create my thoughts, my feelings and my life and I am empowered to be myself again, to unconditionally love and support myself, just the way I am, in all my magnificence.

19. The importance of this affirmation cannot be overemphasized. Say it out loud, and let yourself feel it. Let the words resonate within you. Self-judgment is at the root of all our problems, and even when we have removed judgment from others and forgiven them, we continue to judge ourselves. We even judge ourselves for judging ourselves!

The difficulty we experience in trying to break this cycle results from the fact that the Ego's survival depends on us feeling guilty about who we are. The more successfully we forgive others, the more the Ego tries to compensate by making us feel guilty about ourselves. This explains why we can expect to encounter enormous resistance to moving through the forgiveness process. The Ego feels threatened at every step, and *it will* put up a fight. We see the results of this internal struggle when we do not complete a Forgiveness Worksheet, when we create more reasons to continue projection onto X and feeling victimized, when we do not find time to meditate or forget to do other things that support us in remembering who we are. The closer we get to letting go of something that elicits the feeling of guilt the more the Ego kicks and screams, thus the more difficult the forgiveness process seems.

So, be willing to go through the resistance, knowing that on the other side lies peace and joy. Be willing also to feel any pain, depression, chaos and confusion that might occur while you are going through it.

> 20. I now SURRENDER to the Higher Power I think of as _____*God*_____, and trust in the knowledge that this situation will continue to unfold perfectly and in accordance with Divine guidance and spiritual law. I acknowledge my oneness and feel myself totally reconnected with my Source. I am restored to my true nature, which is LOVE and I now restore love to (X). I close my eyes in order to feel the love that flows in my life and to feel the joy that comes when the love is felt and expressed.

20. This represents the final step in the forgiveness process. However, it is *not* your step to take. You affirm that you are willing to experience it and turn the remainder of the process over to the Higher Power. Ask that the healing be completed by Divine grace and that you and X be restored to your true nature, which is love, and reconnected to your Source which is also Love.

This final step offers you the opportunity to drop the words, the thoughts and the concepts and to actually *feel* the love. When you reach the bottom line, only love exists. If you can truly tap into that love, you are home free. You need do nothing else.

So, take a few minutes to meditate on this statement, and be open to feeling the love. You may have to try this exercise many times before you feel it, but one day, just when you least expect it, the love and the joy will envelop you.

21. A Note To You (X) _____   "Having done this worksheet today, I....

I realize how lucky I am to have you in my life.
I knew we were meant to be together for a reason
and now I know what it was.

I completely forgive you (X) for I now realize that you did nothing wrong and that everything is in Divine order. I acknowledge, accept and love you unconditionally just the way you are.

21. You began the Forgiveness Worksheet by confronting (X) Your energy probably has shifted since you began, even if the shift occurred only a moment or two ago. How do you feel about (X) now? What would you like to say to (X)? Allow yourself to write without conscious thought, if possible, and do not judge your words. Let them surprise even you.

Then, as you acknowledge, accept and love (X) unconditionally just the way he or she is, you recognize and forgive the projection that made you see (X) as less than perfect. You can love (X) without judgment now, because you realize that is the only way a person can be loved. You can love (X) now, because you realize that how he/she appears in the world represents the only way he or she can be. That is how Spirit has willed him or her to be for you.

237

22. A Note To Myself

I honor myself for having the courage to go through this and for being able to get beyond being the victim - I am FREE!

I recognize that I am a spiritual being having a human experience and I love and support myself in every aspect of my humanness.

22. Remember, all forgiveness starts as a lie. You begin the process without forgiveness in your heart, and *you fake it until you make it.* So, honor yourself for doing it and yet be gentle with yourself, and let the forgiveness process take as long as you need. Be patient with yourself. Acknowledge yourself for the courage it takes simply to attempt completing the Forgiveness Worksheet, for you truly face your demons in the process. Doing this work takes enormous courage, willingness and faith.

21: Collapsing the Story

The story is where the pain resides. It is what we write in Box #1 of the worksheet to complete the sentence *'The situation as I see now is....'*

Since it appears to be the source of all our pain and discomfort it is worth turning the spotlight on our victim story to see the extent to which it is real and whether holding on to the pain is justified. We might find that there's very little in it that is actually true. We might find that it is just a story we have created to keep us stuck in separation in order to reinforce our belief that we are not all One. It might also be that we have created this story to give us clues as to what we might be needing to heal (forgive) within ourselves so that we can come to the realization that we are indeed all One.

Obviously it is this last possibility to which Radical Forgiveness gives attention for it is our belief that the very purpose of the story - and of course the role of all the players within it - is to highlight and bring to conscious awareness that which needs healing. It is in the dismantling of the story that we find our opportunity to learn the real truth about ourselves and to remember who we really are.

In the process of tracing back how the story got formed we can usually see how a false negative core belief was first created, then repressed and subsequently made active in the subconscious mind such that it would continue to create circumstances to reinforce itself. This is what happened to Jill. (see Chapter One). Her unconscious core belief was, "I'm not good enough for any man," and she lived it out. Once we collapsed the story and she saw that it was not true, she healed the core belief and everything worked out.

These core beliefs usually form when we are very young. When something happens to us we interpret that experience and give personal meaning to the situation. Then, we confuse what really happened with our interpretation of what happened. The story we *make up* based on that mixture of fact and fiction becomes our truth and an operating principle in our lives.

For example, let's say our father leaves home when we are five years old. For us, this event is traumatic and painful, but in our mind that is only the beginning of our story. At that age we think the world revolves around us so we can only see it from that egocentric point of view. So we make our own interpretations based on that viewpoint. Our first interpretation is that *he left ME!* After that comes many more that expand the story egocentrically, such as: *"It must be my fault. I must have done something to drive him away. He doesn't love me any more. Maybe he never did. I must be a very unlovable person if my father would leave me. He can't care about me and if he doesn't care about me, who will?*

I guess if he doesn't love me nobody will love me, and even if they do they are sure to leave me after five years because that's the way things are with men who say they love you. You can't really trust men who say they love you because they are bound to leave after 5 years anyway. I am just not very lovable. I will never have a relationship that will last more than five years. If I was not good enough for my father, I will never be good enough for anyone."

Fig. 14: How A (False) Story Grows

We might also if we are female, as happened with someone in my workshop recently who had this story running, make it up that men are always subject to being 'stolen' by other women

241

and unconsciously create situations where this happens —
in this example after about five years of being in relationship.

These stories become like internal gyroscopes with their own
frequencies that attract events and people to them so they get
played out according to the beliefs they contain.

But as we can see, the only part of the story that is true is the
original event. Father left. That might be perhaps 5% of the
total story. The rest is simply interpretation — assumptions
made by a very immature frightened mind. That makes the
story 95% B.S! *(Belief System)?*

Your Higher Self knows that those ideas are not only B.S.
but highly toxic as well, so while it cannot intervene directly
since Spirit gave us free will, it brings people into your life
who will lovingly "act out" parts of your story over and over
until you realize that it is not true.

Again, this is what happened with my sister Jill. When our
father demonstrated the kind of love for my daughter,
Lorraine, that Jill always wanted to feel from him and had
not felt, Jill took that to mean that she was inherently unlovable. That became the story she believed until she
brought someone into her life (Jeff) who was able to make
her discover her story and to see that it was false.

Discovering the story is half the battle. Sometimes you are
aware of it, sometimes not. Glenda was a sophisticated,
intelligent, attractive and accomplished woman in her late
forties. She had never been married. In fact, she had never

had a relationship that lasted more than two or three years. It seemed she could never meet *Mr. Right.* Whenever she got to know a man well, she discovered something about him that annoyed her or made her feel dissatisfied with the relationship. So, she would end the relationship. This happened over and over again. She did not see it as a problem, though. As a career woman, she said her job provided her with a lot of satisfaction. On the other hand, she did concede that she was lonely.

One day a good friend asked her, "Have you ever wondered why you don't hold onto a relationship? Have you ever thought that maybe it's not the *something* that you see in them that makes you annoyed or dissatisfied but the *something* in you that you haven't dealt with that won't let you have a decent relationship with a man?"

At the time Glenda just shrugged off her friend's words, but later she began thinking more deeply about her friend's query. She decided to work with a therapist to see if anything lay behind her relationship pattern. The therapist hypnotized her and then regressed her to the age of eight.

Under hypnosis, she recalled that at that age every day she would come home from school to play with her best friend, Mark. They had been close friends since they were very young and were truly inseparable at this point in time. Then she recalled an incident that happened one day after she had changed out of her school clothes and run over to Mark's house. She knocked on the door, and no one answered. She put her face close to the glass and peered

243

in. Her heart sank when she saw the house was empty. Where was everyone? Where was the furniture? Where was Mark? She did not understand—not until she turned to leave the front porch and saw a small sign lying flat in the grass. It said, 'SOLD.'

It slowly dawned on Glenda that Mark's parents had sold the house and gone away taking Mark with them—gone without saying a word, without so much as a good-bye, without even telling her. Mark had never even mentioned that he was moving.

Hurt and confused, Glenda sat on the porch for a few hours before walking the short distance home. She remembered making two decisions during that time. The first was to say nothing to her parents. If they mentioned Mark being gone, she would pretend she did not care. The second decision was never to trust a boy (man) again.

She had apparently forgotten all about this incident, but when it surfaced during her therapy session she became upset. The years of repressed grief over being abandoned by her best friend poured out as did the rage over what she saw as a betrayal.

After the session, she went to see her mother. She talked about Mark and asked her Mother what happened to him and his family. "Oh, his father got transferred," her mother said. "It all happened quite quickly, but we were very surprised that you said nothing about their leaving. We thought you'd be really upset, but you seemed to just take it in your stride. In fact we and Mark's parents talked before they left, because all of us were concerned that you and Mark would be terribly upset. We all agreed it would be best in the long run if we didn't tell either of you anything about the move until the day it actually happened. They didn't even put a For Sale sign up on the house. It was not until Mark was in the car and on the way to their new home that they even told him."

Glenda was stunned. If Mark did not know about the move, then he had not betrayed her after all. At that moment the realization hit her — for more than 30 years she had allowed a completely buried subconscious story to rule her life and to spoil every romantic relationship she had ever had. Not only that, the idea itself was based on a totally false assumption.

As soon as any man got close enough to Glenda to be her friend and her lover, she ended the relationship. She believed that if she got close to a man, like she had been with Mark, he would abandon and betray her in the same way. She was not going to risk suffering that degree of pain again, not for any man. Not only that, she shut down, or suppressed, her feelings of abandonment and betrayal on the day she discovered Mark had moved. Later, she poured herself into her career as a way of avoiding those feelings.

The friend who confronted Glenda with her self-defeating pattern saw beyond her *story* and recognized that something else was going on. She had created many healing opportunities but had missed them all.

245

Glenda came to a Radical Forgiveness workshop and forgave the man with whom she had separated most recently and, as a consequence, all the others that she had judged as 'not trustworthy' before him. That automatically neutralized the original idea that she could never trust a man again so she became free to have the relationship that she really wanted.

Unlike Glenda, Jesse, another workshop participant, appeared fully aware of her story but still did not see the mistake in it. This was in spite of the fact that she was spiritually very aware. She was at one of my workshops and told us that she had just been fired from her job. "That's OK," she said, "It's my abandonment issue playing itself out again. I get fired or lose a relationship every couple of years. It's because I was abandoned when I was a baby."

I suspected a B.S. story so I began to investigate the abandonment. What we soon discovered was that her father had died just before she was born and that her mother had become ill when Jesse was about two years old and unable to cope. Consequently, Jesse was reared for a while by her grandparents.

Though she was no doubt traumatized by being separated from her mother, the actual truth of the matter was that her parents never did abandon her. They were simply absent and through no fault of their own. They certainly did not abandon her. To abandon someone is to make a calculated and conscious choice to leave them. It is a deliberate act. Mere absence does not constitute abandonment.

Taking absence to mean abandonment was an interpretation that a small child might easily make and yet the importance goes way beyond semantics. Interpreting her parent's
absence as abandonment, she went on to make a number
of other interpretations such as: *"If my parents abandon
me, then I must be a very unlovable person. No one
will ever stay with me for more than 2 years because,
if my mother abandons me after that time, everyone
will do exactly that. They won't want me after that.
They will realize that I am a bad person and will leave.
That's how life is."*

Jesse had been living out of this particular story for all her
52 years. Yet it was founded on a complete misinterpreta-
tion of the situation. Once she saw that, she was able to
let it go and become free from the need to create abandonment every two years from that point on.

Even though she had spiritual awareness, she had consistently failed to realize that in providing instances of abandonment every two years, Spirit was in fact giving her opportunities to wake up and heal a toxic story which was a
limitation on her life and a wound to her soul. Doing some
forgiveness worksheets on the person who had last fired
her helped her clear all the other times she had been 'abandoned' over her 52 years and neutralized her original abandonment story.

The Forgiveness Centrifuge

Using this tool might have saved both Jill, Jesse and Glenda many years of painful struggle. The Forgiveness Centrifuge helps us separate *what actually happened* in any given situation from our *interpretation* of what happened. If you own the type of juicer where you put carrots and other things in the top and the juice is separated from the fiber by the centrifugal force of the spinning grater, you know what is meant by the term centrifuge. A centrifuge also is used to separate blood from plasma, cream from milk, and so on. A washing machine spinning out the excess water from clothes works in the same manner as well.

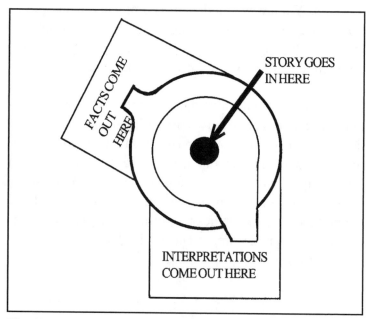

Fig. 15: Separating Fact From Fiction

A forgiveness centrifuge simply reverses the process by which we come up with stories about what happened to us. To use it, take the story you are living now — the one that is causing you discomfort. Remember, it is certain to be a hopeless mixture of fact (what happened) and interpretation (all your thoughts, judgments, assessments, assumptions, and beliefs about what happened). Feed the story into the top of the imaginary centrifuge, just like you would with carrots in a juicer, and then, in your mind, see the machine separating the facts from the interpretations.

Then, like any good researcher, first make a list of the facts as they emerge, being as objective as possible. Then make a list of the interpretations you made about the facts.

#	The Facts About What Happened

After writing down your results, acknowledge the facts and accept them. Recognize that the facts tell what happened and that no one can do anything to change that. You have no choice but to allow what happened to be exactly what happened, but watch for any tendency to make excuses for what happened. This to impose interpretation on the facts once again. Just stay with what actually happened. Next, examine every thought, belief, rationalization, idea, or attitude you imposed on what happened, and declare them all to be *untrue*. Affirm that none of them have validity. Tell yourself they just represent mind-talk.

#	My Interpretations About What Happened

Then, recognize how important your ideas, beliefs and attitudes are to you. Look at your *attachment* to each of them, and decide which of them you possibly are ready to drop and which you are not.

	Interpretations	% Attachment

Be Gentle With Yourself

Do not criticize yourself for being attached to any of them or for being unwilling to let them go. You may have had these ideas, beliefs and attitudes for a long time. In fact, they may define who you are. For example, if you are an incest survivor or an adult child of an alcoholic, these labels, which represent ideas or beliefs about yourself, may

251

provide a reference for who you are. If you let go of the ideas associated with these labels, you might lose your identity. So, while you want to be firm with yourself in separating what is real from what you have made up, be gentle with yourself and allow time to release these beliefs.

The next step after this is the Radical Forgiveness reframe — seeing that the story was perfect and had to play out that way. Watch out for the guilt, the anger, the depression, and the criticism you might feel and direct at yourself when you find out you have created your entire life around a set of untrue beliefs. *Please, do not do this*. Instead, remember that everything has a purpose, and God does not make mistakes. Use one or more of the forgiveness tools to work on forgiving yourself and on seeing the perfection in your situation.

If the facts still prove that something *bad* took place — for example, a murder remains a murder no matter what interpretations you may have made, the Radical Forgiveness Worksheet provides the best tool to help you shift the energy around that event.

22: Four Steps to Forgiveness

This adaptation of a three-step process taught by Arnold Patent, serves as a reminder of our power to attract the events and people we need to feel the emotions we have around a particular issue.

This process takes only a few moments but it is one that literally could save you from getting totally caught up in the drama of what is happening and going to *'Victimland'* for an extended stay!

When something happens and we get upset it is extremely easy for us to forget everything we ever knew about Radical Forgiveness. Until these principles become firmly anchored in our minds our tendency is always to default to victim consciousness whenever our upset creates a lot of emotional turmoil. The problem is, once there, we tend to hang out there for a very long time. Without a Radical Forgiveness viewpoint you would probably stay there for years, which is what most people do. *(See diagram next page)*. However if you have someone who knows Radical Forgiveness and recognizes your symptoms, they will have

---

* Patent A. M. *"You Can Have It All"* Simon & Schuster, 1995 and *"Death Taxes And Other Illusions"* (Celebration Publishing, 1989).

you do a worksheet or listen to the 13 Steps CD so you can return to peace. As you will see on the diagram below, each time something happens we default to becoming a victim and go for an extended stay in *victimland.* Then we get reminded of how everything might be perfect so we use the technology to express our willingness to see the perfection and eventually return to a state of peace.

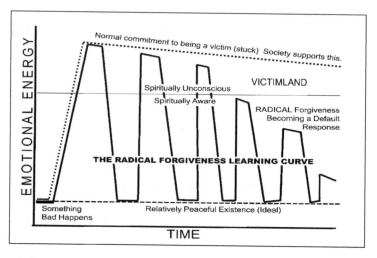

Fig. 16: The Victimland Roller-coaster

However, this can be a rough ride and it depends on your having someone who will rescue you. The way to stop this roller-coaster is to use the 4-step process ***before*** you have to book yourself a room in *victimland!* On the diagram this is represented by the curves that stop just short of the line at which we usually go unconscious. When we find ourselves doing this naturally as a matter of course then Radical Forgiveness has become our default life-style — thanks to the 4-Step Process.

So, as soon as you find yourself getting upset over something, or even if you find yourself making judgments, feeling self-righteous or wanting to change something about a situation, use this process to bring your consciousness back into alignment with the principles of Radical Forgiveness.

Step One: *"Look what I created!"*

This first step reminds us that we are the creators of our reality. However, we create circumstances for our own healing, so do not assume *guilt* for what happens. Being quick to judge, we often use this step as a way to *beat ourselves up.* We say, "Look what I have created. Oh, it's terrible — I must be a terrible person, a spiritual failure." Please do not fall into this trap, for if you do, you buy into the illusion.

Step Two: *"I notice my judgments and love myself for having them."*

This step acknowledges that as humans we automatically attach a whole string of judgments, interpretations, questions, and beliefs to situations. Our task involves accepting the imperfection of our own humanity and loving ourselves for having these judgments, including the one that says we must be a spiritually-moribund person for creating this reality. Our judgments are part of ourselves, so we must love them as ourselves. This connects us with what actually is happening in our body and mind and brings us into the present through our feelings. Our energy then shifts quickly and allows us to go to the third and fourth steps of this process.

255

Step Three: *"I am willing to see the perfection in the situation."*

The *willingness* step is the essential step in the Radical Forgiveness process. It equates to a prayerful surrendering in the moment to the Divine plan and the willingness to love ourselves for not being able to see this plan directly.

Step Four: *"I choose the power of peace."*

This fourth step represents a consequence of all the previous steps. By accepting that Divine purpose is served in this situation and that what appears to be occurring may be illusionary, we choose to feel peace and to use the power of peace in whatever actions are required of us. The power of peace is found when we are totally present in the moment, acting with clarity and focus to do whatever may be required and totally aware of our feelings.

Practice this four-step process as often as possible. Make it a part of your awareness. It gives you a way to be in the moment throughout your day.

To help you make this your practice, it is a good idea to put these four steps on a business size card for your purse or wallet, or on a 3"x 5" card to keep on your refrigerator.

Note: *The previous printing featured an **Epilogue on 9/11** which demonstrated the use of the 4-step process in such a situation. This is now archived on my web site. At the Home page, click on 'America's Healing.' You will find it there - along with a lot more good stuff on this, Saddam and other topics.*

23: Seeing the Christ in Another

If you recognize that a situation occurring between you and someone else represents an opportunity to heal something in yourself, you can create the healing experience by being totally in that present moment. A way to bring your energy into present time, as opposed to allowing your mind to be in the past or in the future, requires simply looking at the person with whom you are having an issue and *seeing the Christ in them.*

In this sense, the term *Christ* means the part of them that is Divine and one with you and with God. As you do this, you join with them, and in that moment, you acknowledge the Christ within you. If you have the presence of mind to do this, you will transform the situation immediately.

When we truly join with another person and become one with them, we transcend the Ego. The Ego's whole existence is based on separation. Without separation, we have no need to attack and defend — so in that moment of joining we raise our vibration, drop all our mechanisms of defense and become our true selves. At the same time we let go of our projections and see the other person as a child of God, perfect in every sense. This is the essence of Radical Forgiveness.

Seeing the Christ in Ourselves

It is important to recognize that the mechanism of projection does not just apply to the shadow side of us. We also project onto other people the things we like about ourselves yet have a hard time acknowledging. Thus we see in those people our own inner beauty, our own creative talent, our own intelligence and so on.

The Positive Reflection Exercise

This is an exercise taught by Arnold Patent and is powerful in its effect on everyone who tries it, because it asks you to see, first, what is wonderful in another person, and second, to claim that quality as your own. It truly connects people with their essence — with the Christ in themselves — and allows them to really see who they are. The exercise is usually done in a group setting, but it can equally be done with two people. It is similar to seeing the Christ in a person, but instead of doing it silently, this is done verbally and with eye contact.

Person A, speaking from the heart, says to person B, "The beautiful, wonderful qualities that I see in you, that you reflect in me, are..." Person A, then tells the person the qualities they see. Person B, listens and responds by saying, "Thank you." They then switch over and repeat the exercise.

24: Forgiveness Is a 3-Letter Word

This tool simply involves writing three letters to the person you feel has wronged or hurt you in some way. It works wonderfully when you are really upset about something that has just happened or even on something that may have happened a long time ago.

Vent all your anger and rage in the first letter. Hold nothing back. You can threaten vengeance of the vilest kind if it makes you feel good. Keep writing until you have nothing left to say. The process of writing this letter may cause you to shed a lot of tears — tears of rage, sadness, resentment, and hurt. Let them flow. Have a box of tissues beside you. If you are angry, scream into a pillow or do some physical activity to help you feel your anger. *Under no circumstances mail this letter!*

The next day, write another letter. This one should carry somewhat less anger and vengeance, although it still does not let the person with whom you are angry off the hook for what you believe they have done to you. However, it should make an effort to bring compassion, understanding, and generosity, as well as the possibility of some sort of forgiveness, into the equation. *Do not mail this letter either.*

The following day, write a third letter. In this one, attempt to describe a new interpretation of the situation based on the principles of Radical Forgiveness. Since this mimics the forgiveness worksheet, refer to the notes on the worksheet to give you the signposts for your letter, but write it in your own words as best you can. (See Chapter 20.) This may feel like a struggle at first, but persevere. Remember, you will have to fake it for a while before you make it.

None of these letters are ever mailed. It is neither necessary nor desirable to mail them. They are designed to shift *your* energy, not the energy of the recipient. Venting your feelings, rather than projecting them once again onto the other person serves as the objective. Sending the angry letter, in particular, accomplishes nothing whatsoever. Doing so would only keep the attack-defense cycle going on and on, and that would drag you deeper into the drama. Remember, as you shift your energy in the direction of Radical Forgiveness, the energy of the other person changes automatically.

You either can keep the letters for future reference, or you can use them in a forgiveness ritual. My personal preference lies in using the ritual of fire to transform them. Something powerful happens when you see your words turn into ashes and rise up in a column of smoke.

25: Forgiveness Rituals

The power of ritual is underestimated in our society today. When we ritualize any procedure we make it sacred, thus the ritual speaks directly to our soul. While rituals can be very simple or quite complex, the complexity matters less than the reverence you show the ritual. The ritual invites the participation of the Divine in human affairs and as such, represents another way of praying.

Rituals become all the more powerful when we create them ourselves. When devising your own rituals, be as creative as you can. However, here are some general guidelines and ideas you may want to use.

Ritual with Fire

Fire has always been the element of transformation and alchemy. Whenever we offer something up through fire, we tap into primordial beliefs in fire's transformative power. For this reason, a ritual burning of a forgiveness worksheet, a release letter or the letter trilogy provides a sense of completion and transformation. Carry out the burning with ceremony and with reverence. Say a prayer as the item burns.

Burning scented woods, sage, sweetgrass, and incense will intensify any ritual and bring special significance to a forgiveness ceremony. The smoke from sage and sweet grass also cleanses your aura; thus removing unwanted energies from your energy field.

Ritual with Water

Water possesses healing and cleansing qualities, and we give it the ability to make things holy. Ritualized washing, immersing and floating all can be used to good effect. For example, instead of burning a release letter, fold it into a boat and let a fast flowing stream of water take it away.

Be creative with your rituals, and make them meaningful to you. You may recall the story of Jane who had brain cancer and had put in the attic a box containing everything associated with a man who broke her heart. I asked her to take the box down from the attic and bring it with her to therapy. Had she not had a seizure and died before we could do so, we would have gone through the box examining every item in it and what it meant to her. Then, we would have disposed of them one by one with a ritual bearing meaning for her. This process would have released much repressed energy.

26: Artful Forgiveness

Art provides a powerful tool for forgiveness and emotional release. One of the most dramatic healings through art I have ever been privileged to witness and/or to participate in, occurred at the retreat I did in England. One of the participants was a young woman with multiple sclerosis. Her body was weak and wasted, and her voice was hardly audible. Her throat chakra was virtually shut down. She had a husband and two children, but the marriage was basically non-existent and she felt trapped, helpless and hopeless.

At one point during a group art therapy session, she began to draw in a particularly unique fashion. She could not talk, but she kept drawing and drawing. It was hard to discern what she was drawing, but it became clear over time that she was using the medium as a way to regress herself and release old childhood pain.

My wife and I sat there with her as she drew hour after hour, her drawings becoming more and more child-like as time went on. In addition to her pictures, occasionally she would scrawl phrases like, *bad girl,* and *God doesn't love me,* and other words indicating deep shame, guilt and fear. Finally, she made a crude stick drawing of what she later recalled as childhood rape by an uncle. In this cathartic release, she was able to express in drawings what she had found it impossible to say in words and sounds. Her throat chakra had shut down because of what she was forced to do with her mouth. (Her uncle had made her have oral sex with him.) Suddenly, art became an outlet for memories and emotions that had remained repressed for many years. These memories and emotions were responsible for her illness.

To support this woman in her catharsis, my wife went to the far end of the rather large room in which we were holding the retreat. We then asked her to use her voice to tell my wife that she was a *good girl,* and that *God loved her.* I made her do it louder and louder until she was shouting at the top of her lungs. After she had shouted, *God loves me,* about 20 times, she stopped and looked at me and affirmed, "He really does love me, doesn't he?!" That healing moment I will never forget.

Three months after we got back from England, we received a letter from her saying she had left her husband, had gotten a new place to live and had found a job. She was using her voice and asking for what she wanted, and she was finding that she had the power, not only to ask, but also to receive. She had even started a support group for people with multiple sclerosis and was doing art therapy with them. Her strength was returning day by day, and after three years, we still hear from her and marvel at her continuously increasing strength.

If you are not a verbally inclined person and are not comfortable writing things down, try drawing. You may be surprised what will happen when you communicate in this manner. Buy some decently sized white and black paper as well as some colored pastel chalks and crayons. (The pastels work really well on the black paper.)

Know that to use this tool requires no artistic talent whatsoever. It is not about painting pretty pictures. In fact, if you are full of anger, your pictures will probably be anything but pretty. It is about getting emotions and thoughts out on paper.

Begin drawing with no expectations or preconceived ideas. You might ask God or your spirit guides to help you release through the process of drawing and coloring whatever needs releasing, and then simply start. Whatever wants to come, allow it. Do not judge. Just go with the flow. Do this like a meditation. If you want to tell a story, do that. If you just want to use color, do that. Do whatever you feel like doing.

To use art therapy as a forgiveness tool, use an approach similar to that of the letter trilogy. Do a series of drawings that express how you felt about what a particular person did to you; these pictures would express your anger, fear, pain, sadness, etc. Then, move into a more compassionate and understanding frame of mind, and do some drawings that reflect this attitude. Do a third set that expresses the feeling of Radical Forgiveness. You might want to put some time between each phase, or you can do them all in the same sitting. Make sure, however, that once you start doing this art therapy, you complete all three stages — even if you only do three drawings in all. Doing just the first one, for example, might leave you stuck in anger.

As you finish each picture, hang it on a wall. Place each picture in the precise order in which you complete them, and create a vertical or horizontal band on the wall with them. If you are creating a vertical display, begin with the first of the angry ones at the bottom and end with the last Radical Forgiveness one at the top. When you place them in such a manner, you will be amazed to see the progression and the change in the quality of the energy expressed by each picture.

Title each drawing and date it. Spend some time with the drawings. Let them "speak" to you. While you were drawing each picture, you were thinking certain thoughts. When you look at the drawing later, clear your mind of those thoughts and examine the pictures for anything else of importance. Invite others you trust to give you their interpretations of the pictures. They may see things you do not. Ask for their input by saying, "If this were your picture, what would you see?" If what they see resonates with you, fine. If it does not really ring true for you, that is fine too. They see into your drawing through their own subconscious, not yours, but you will find that people's observations will trigger within you a whole new way of looking at your drawings, and you may have some new insights as a result.

266

27: Satori Breathwork

As we have discussed previously, suppressed or repressed emotions have toxic effects on both our mental and physical health. Releasing these emotions serves as the first step in the forgiveness process. We can release held emotions the most quickly and the most effectively by using a process called Satori Breath. (Satori is a Japanese word meaning *insight* or *awakening*.)

Satori breathwork is usually done lying on your back and involves breathing with full awareness in a circular pattern. In other words, you consciously breathe in a manner that has no pause between the in-breath and the out-breath. Carefully selected music is played rather loudly throughout the process.

The person breathes for between 40 to 60 minutes through an open mouth, sometimes long and deep into the abdomen, and at other times fast and shallow into the upper chest. This oxygenates the body to such an extent that the body releases from its cells suppressed emotion that has crystallized into energy particles within the cells. As these energy particles are released, the person often becomes consciously aware of these old feelings in present time.

The feelings may be expressed as pure emotion, such as sadness, anger or despair, unattached to any memory associated with them. Conversely, the memory of an event, idea, association or misperception that caused the emotion to be felt and suppressed in the first place may come sharply into focus. It may even surface in a symbolic way or in the form of a metaphor. On the other hand, there may be no conscious recall of anything. For each person and in each breathing session, the experience is different as well as impossible to predict.

As emotions come up, the person *breathes through* them, which allows the person not only to feel them fully but to release them. We often stop breathing to hold emotions in check; therefore, breathing through them allows us to feel them and release them. In some cases, the person expresses them verbally and kinesthetically while breathing. No matter how the emotions are released, almost invariably a sense of profound calm and deep peace results from the process.

This simple technique provides dramatic and long-lasting healing effects. I have no hesitation in recommending this work to anyone who is serious about wanting to clear out their emotional closet.

The effects of Satori Breathwork are profound precisely because they happen totally within the person without any interjection, guidance, steering, or manipulation whatsoever by the facilitator. In fact, a facilitator only is present to *hold the space as safe* and to support the breather in moving through the feelings — which sometimes can be scary — rather than suppressing them again. I would not recommend that you do this process on your own for that reason.

Conscious connected breathing is also called *rebirthing,* because researchers have found that breathwork gives us access to memories and emotions lodged in our cells as early as during our in-utero experience, during the actual birth process and soon after the birth. Birth represents our first major life trauma, and we form profound ideas about struggle, abandonment, safety and acceptance as we go through this experience. These ideas often become beliefs that literally run our lives. When someone re-experiences their birth and releases the traumas and beliefs they formed at that time, their lives change dramatically.

Another great benefit of Satori Breathwork comes from the fact that it integrates new energy patterns into our existing energy fields and restructures our subtle bodies accordingly. This means that when you shift your perception, have an insight or release old emotional patterns, breathwork integrates this into your body's data banks. Using the computer analogy, it is as if breathwork serves as a downloading process where data currently stored in the short-term computer memory is transferred to the hard drive for permanent storage.

This also explains why Satori Breathwork becomes so important in the Radical Forgiveness process. It accomplishes these tasks, not just at the beginning of the process

269

for the purpose of emotional release, but afterwards too, when our belief systems change and all the resulting changes in our energy fields need integrating. The integration process anchors the changes in our bodies and helps prevent us from going back to our old ways.

I would suggest that you have between 10 and 20 supervised breathing sessions over a period of time, which may take up to a year. After that, you can probably do the breathing process on your own.

28: The Release Letter

The Release Letter is an adaptation of a letter given to me by hypnotherapist and mind/body therapist, Dr. Sharon Forrest of the Forrest Foundation, a non-profit corporation dedicated to alternative holistic healing, located in Mexico.

The Release Letter proclaims to your Higher Self and to every part of your being that you give full permission for all aspects of unforgiveness still remaining in any situation to be lovingly released.

It also serves as an instrument of self-forgiveness, for it recognizes that you have created the experiences as a way to learn and to grow.

Photocopy the letter as written on the following page and enlarge it to an appropriate size.

To use the Release Letter, fill in the blanks, have it witnessed by someone and then burn it in a ritual manner.

Release Letter

Date: _____ Name _____

Dear Higher Self:

I, _____ , hereby grant you, my Higher Self, my Soul, my Super-Conscious Mind, my DNA, my cellular memory, and all parts of myself that might want to hold onto the unforgiveness for whatever reason, permission to release all of the misunderstandings, unfounded beliefs, misinterpretations, and misguided emotions, wherever they may reside, whether in my body, my unconscious mind, my DNA, my conscious mind, my subconsious mind, my unconscious mind, my chakras and even my Soul, and I ask all those who want the best for me to assist in this releasing process.

I, _____ , thank you, my Soul, for creating the experiences that created the unforgiveness and realize that on some level they have all been my teachers and have offered opportunites for me to learn and to grow. I accept the experiences, without judgment and do hereby release them to the nothingness from which they came.

I, _____ , do hereby forgive _____

I release him/her to their highest good and set him/her free. I bless him/her for having been willing to be my teacher. I sever all unhealthy attachments to this person and send him/her unconditional love and support.

I, _____ , do hereby forgive myself, and accept myself just the way I am and love myself unconditionally just the way I am, in all my power and magnificence.

I, _____ , do hereby release myself to my highest good and claim for myself freedom, fulfilment of my dreams, wishes and goals, clarity, love, full expression, creativity, health and prosperity.

Signed: _____ Date: _____

Witnessed by: _____ Date: _____

272

29: The Forgiveness Rose

When we open our hearts to others, we become vulnerable and face the danger of becoming the target for their projections. Their psychic energy can become mixed with ours, and this can deplete our energy.

The more workshops I do the more I realize that in many cases the problems people appear to be having with someone in particular stem from the fact that that person is able to get into and manipulate their energy field. Almost invariably they seem to be entering through the third chakra which is the one where all our issues of power and control are stored. Once in, they find it easy to control us. They can suck our energy or dump theirs onto us at will.

Of course, this is all done subconsciously - without awareness and hopefully without malice - but it can be debilitating to the one being manipulated and puts a great strain on the relationship.

You probably won't be surprised to learn that it is most often the person's mother who is doing the invading and controlling - even from the grave I might add. It might also be the father or the spouse or any other person who wants to have some control over your life, but most often it is the mother.

The easiest way to stop this or to prevent it happening with other people you come in contact with, is to simply put up an imaginary rose between you and the other person. It is a surprisingly powerful protective device.

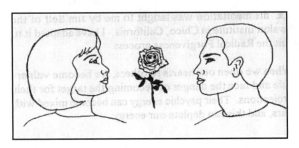

Fig. 17: The Rose.

The rose is a symbol of psychic protection in a great many esoteric writings. For whatever reason, it possesses a great deal of potency in this regard probably because it is the universal symbol for love. Visualizing a rose gives us protection from the projections of others, offering a way to block negative energy without closing our heart to the person. I cannot explain why the rose visualization works so well in this regard; in truth, we can create psychic protection with any kind of visualization, because just doing so creates the intention of self protection. However, the rose has been used for centuries for this purpose and seems to work better than most other symbols.

So from now on, any time you encounter someone whose energy you don't want mixed with your own, visualize the rose existing at the edge of your aura, or halfway between yourself and the person. Then notice if you feel differently while in their presence. You should feel a much greater sense of your own psychic space and identity while at the same time being totally present for the person. You don't have to be in someone's physical presence for them to be able to control your energy so it is a good idea to put up your rose even while talking on the phone.

If you wish to develop this skill further we do offer a CD, available from our web site, entitled, "The Satori Grounding Meditation." This takes you through a short guided meditation in which you learn how to, prior to putting up the rose, ground your energy, bring your own energy field under your control and then balance the energy in each of the chakras.

You can use this every day to create your 'protection' rose for the day, as well as balance all your chakras. At night, just before you go to bed you put everything that happened that day into your rose and blow it up — or *dissolve* it if you prefer to visualize it that way.

We also have available a CD that uses the rose technique in the process of forgiveness. You would use this when the need arose to forgive someone. It is entitled *"The Rose Forgiveness Meditation."*

275

30: RADICAL *Self*-Forgiveness

W e have learned in the foregoing chapters, I hope, that whatever we see *out there* is an outpicturing of what is *in here,* and that what we see in other people is simply a reflection of our own consciousness. If you are one of a crowd of two thousand people crammed into a room, there is, in reality, only one person in the room — and it is you. The rest of the people are reflections of you and your perception of them is simply a story that you have made up in your mind. We are always looking in the mirror and it's all about us. In the same way therefore, ***all*** forgiveness is self-forgiveness.

This is what I have been arguing for a long time. Self-forgiveness happens by default as soon as your realize that what you see *out there,* is you. *(See steps 9 thru 12 on the worksheet).* Once we see the truth in someone, we automatically claim it for ourselves.

It always seemed to me to be easier to forgive what was *out there,* rather than to try forgiving oneself, because we are accustomed to operating in the world as either subject or object, but never both at the same time — which is how it is with self-forgiveness. To whom are we appealing when we ask ourselves for forgiveness? Who would be forgiving whom? No wonder self-forgiveness is so difficult — we are trying to be judge, jury, defendant and witness all in the same case! Better (perhaps) that we do it by radically forgiving others and, in so doing, vicariously and automatically forgiving ourselves at the same time.

This is all the more true since much of what we do hate in ourselves is unconscious and therefore hidden from us. How can we forgive in ourselves that about which we know nothing? Fortunately, as we know, the Law of Attraction helps us out by bringing someone into our lives who will resonate those issues for us and mirror them back to us. Initially, of course, it upsets us greatly but as we do the worksheet and forgive them *(see the truth)*, we automatically forgive ourselves. That is why we say that the people we judge and dislike the most are our greatest teacher and healers.

Another reason why I resisted doing self-forgiveness work was that I had noticed that many of those who tended to want to work on forgiving themselves, rather than on forgiving others, were often addicted to self-blame and recrimination. These people would jump at the chance to use self-forgiveness as simply another way to continue beating themselves up. By our insisting that they begin by first forgiving others, we not only broke their denial about not having issues with other people *(which, of course, they always did),* but enabled them to find genuine self-forgiveness through the normal Radical Forgiveness process.

Having said all that, I do recognize that there is still a need to provide the context and the spaciousness for connecting with, and extending mercy and forgiveness towards, those parts of ourselves that have assumed guilt about something that happened and/or feel shame about who we imagine ourselves to be.

For the past year, I have experimented with a self-forgiveness workshop entitled *Emergence,* and have finally proven it to be a beautiful and profoundly healing experience. Let me stress, however, that the context for this self-forgiveness work remains exactly the same as with Radical Forgiveness — that, from a spiritual viewpoint, there is no right or wrong; there are no such things as victims and perpetrators, and that there is, therefore, nothing to forgive. Consequently, the energy release obtained by virtually every participant was real and significant.

An important part of the more advanced self-forgiveness work that I am now offering has its roots in a spiritually oriented therapeutic system known as Psychosynthesis. This was founded and developed in the early 1900's by Roberto Assagioli, an Italian psychiatrist. He was way in advance of his time and is only now being fully recognized and appreciated for the work he did. I am also finding it to be quite consistent with the principles of Radical Forgiveness.

Assagioli's work showed that we have within us not just a singular inner child, as has been popularly represented, but a whole host of subpersonalities. Most of

279

them were created as a way to manage or survive our primal wounds or compensate for our perceived deficiencies — the basis of our injured sense of self.

[I should add that even people who were raised in seemingly healthy families can also be wounded. Often wounding is subtle and can even be the result of a misperception. Spiritual wounding, too, can occur as a result of otherwise nurturing parents being themselves disconnected from Spirit or presenting God as an external entity, separate from ourselves, thereby being unable to impart a spiritual connection.]

Assagioli showed that in order to get beyond these wounds and to expand into the fullness of our potential, we need to make an *empathic connection* with each of them so they can reveal themselves to us, be understood and then forgiven — in the Radical Forgiveness sense, of course. *(Caroline Myss uses a somewhat similar approach with her archetypes, as does Hal Stone with his voice dialogue technique, and David Quigley with his Alchemical Hypnotherapy).*

Earlier, it had been my intention to write another book and for it to be on the subject of self-forgiveness, but once I began writing, I realized that besides this kind of academic content, it would have been very much like this book. That's because basically, I would have been simply substituting the word perpetrator for the word victim, and that's about all the difference it would have made. Of course, there's other content that I could have added too, about dealing with and healing your own shadow, similar to that which Debbie Ford has done so well, but as far as Radical Forgiveness is concerned, it would still have been highly repetitive.

After having done several *Emergence* workshops and having become better acquainted with Assagioli's work, I realized that I needed to create, in addition to the workshops, an **on-line**, internet based, Radical Self-forgiveness Program that people could do in their own homes and yet achieve the same kind of results. That's what we have done.

Earlier, I raised the question regarding who is forgiving whom? Well, there are actually two answers to that question. In the case of traditional forgiveness, the appeal is to the human self or Ego — from the Ego. Clearly, we truly are, in this instance, trying to be judge, jury, defendant and witness all in the same case. That's why it is never successful. The courtroom inside our heads remains in chaos and perpetual deadlock. I am sure many of you know what that feels like.

It is totally different with Radical Self-forgiveness. The appeal here is made, not to our human self at all, but to our Higher Self; our *I Am* consciousness. This is the transcendent part of ourself that is not separate from the All-That-Is, and yet is always there with us at the core of our being, observing us from above, so to speak. It is also the one that knows the truth about there being no right or wrong, good or bad, and does not identify with the content or process of our life in the least. It simply observes — and its gift to me is my self-awareness.

The purpose of the Radical Self-forgiveness process, as I have come to see it, and have it reflected in our workshops and on-line programs, is multifaceted. In the first instance its purpose is to help us understand the nature of *self* and our relationship with those many aspects of ourselves that constitute who we are. We need first to be able to identify and then find a way to relate empathically to the various parts of ourselves that make up who we are, especially those who experienced a shortfall in their nurturing during the formative years.

Once we have identified our wounded subpersonalities and understood their need to exist as survival subpersonalities, or compensate for their perceived deficiencies, we then need to help them move beyond the wound and see the perfection in the circumstances that caused the wounding in the first place. Then we will be free to expand into who we were meant to be and come into the full realization of who we truly are. Only then will we feel unconditional love and acceptance for ourselves.

That will have brought us into full alignment with our transcendent self which knows our pure I AM perfection on the one hand and recognizes on the other, the very perfection in our imperfection.

Then we can say with full understanding of its meaning: "I'm not OK; you're not OK — but that's OK!"

Afterword

Not withstanding the fact that there are some 284 pages separating the Foreword from this Afterword, you will notice that this is a continuation of the same theme that characterized the Foreword — *change*. In the Foreword, I talked about the changes that had occurred up to the time of writing. In this Afterward, the emphasis is on *what's next,* given the fact that I have finally caught up with my own thinking about Radical Forgiveness' being something much larger than a mere process of forgiveness — bigger, in fact, than I ever imagined.

I have known from the beginning that Radical Forgiveness has never been about forgiveness per se — at least, not forgiveness as we have traditionally conceived of it. Neither is it merely an alternative way of forgiving that is quicker or more effective than any other form of forgiveness.

Though it is that, it is also something infinitely greater, more all-encompassing and more revolutionary. It is nothing less than a mind-blowing idea that shatters our existing ideas of reality and challenges our current world view. It invites us to engage in a process that is rooted in 4th dimensional reality which we don't yet understand. Neither is there much proof of its efficacy other than the evidence of our own awareness of how significantly changed we become when we engage in it. *(If you've done a worksheet, you'll know what I mean).*

283

It requires that we suspend our normal way of thinking about ourselves and our relationship to the world at large, and to be open to the possibility that we can begin operating from this new reality *(before we really know what it is or how it works),* by just being willing to do it.

But the truly amazing gift that it offers humanity lies in its capacity to serve as a bridge — a bridge that enables us to move freely and easily, *without knowing it,* between third dimensional reality and fourth dimensional reality. A bridge that enables us to *practice* operating from the love vibration of the latter while existing physically in the former.

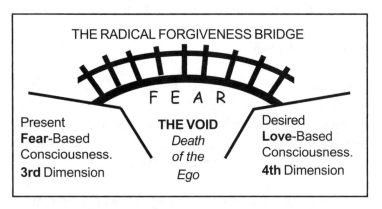

THE RADICAL FORGIVENESS BRIDGE

F E A R

Present
Fear-Based
Consciousness.
3rd Dimension

THE VOID
Death
of the
Ego

Desired
Love-Based
Consciousness.
4th Dimension

Such a bridge is necessary because even though deep down, we know that fourth dimensional reality is based on love, peace, oneness and joy — and we yearn desperately to go there — we are terrified at the thought of letting go of that which is all so familiar. This is true despite that fact that the current reality is one based on fear, separation and pain. The doubt is real and deep seated — what if I jump into the void and find that the other reality doesn't exist after all!

284

So, while the technology of Radical Forgiveness ostensibly appears to be about helping us forgive ourselves and others, its *real* purpose is in giving us a chance to *practice* being in that other reality while being blissfully ignorant of our actual presence there. It lulls us into thinking that we are simply doing a forgiveness worksheet or one of the other processes, when in fact we are, without realizing it, actually stepping across that chasm and operating in fourth dimensional reality. By the use of *smoke and mirrors* and the blessing of ignorance, our Ego happily goes along with the process.

Like anything else, the more we practice something the less fear we have about it. When the time comes for us to make the shift—which I believe is imminent—we will be so used to being in the vibration of the love-based reality (through using Radical Forgiveness), that our fears about making the final leap will have evaporated.

This brings me to a question that people frequently ask having just completed one of my workshops. *"How can I stay in the Radical Forgiveness vibration and not get pulled back into victim consciousness by the world around me?"*

The quick answer is simple—keep using the tools. Each and every time we do it, we become more and more anchored in the fourth dimensional reality and, in turn, it will become less and less likely that we will choose to return to the third. Eventually, it will become our *default* way of being and we will have become fully stabilized at the higher vibratory rate.

But there is a much deeper aspect to this question that we must also address. In order to keep using the tools so that we remain playing in fourth dimensional reality and raising our vibration, *we must stay AWAKE.*

Referring to the diagram on page 254, *(Chapter 22, Fig 16)*, we see from this that, if we become upset to the degree that we go above the line that marks both the loss of spiritual consciousness and that we have crossed into Victimland, we are in deep trouble. The result is a dramatic lowering of our vibratory rate and the loss of awareness of the new-found reality. We find ourselves back in the world of separation and fear-based reality — back in the grip of the Ego. The furthest thing from our mind at this point is doing a worksheet or listening to the 13 Steps. In short, we are lost.

I now see this phenomenon not just as a set-back for the people who lose what they gained through the Radical Forgiveness experience, as the question implied might happen, but as the thing most likely to impede the achievement of the mission to create a world of forgiveness by 2012.

As you know, a certain critical mass of people with their consciousness sufficiently raised to counteract the many whose vibratory rate remains low, is required to create the Awakening. It is critical therefore that all those who have had their vibration raised *(even by reading this book),* remain awake and engaged in the very process that keeps them traversing that bridge.

Until now, my primary goal in using Radical Forgiveness has been on healing our wounds and releasing energy blocks in order to improve our lives. Not that I have restricted it to working with individuals for I have found it to be every bit as potent a technology for healing communities.

Working in Australia gave me the opportunity to try it in the context of the reconciliation movement that is happening there as white and aboriginal Australians come together to heal their terrible past. I wrote and published a book there called *Reconciliation Through Radical Forgiveness, A Spiritual Technology for Healing Communities.* This book was designed to give everyone in Australia who wanted reconciliation, the spiritual technology to bring it about — something they could use in their own homes, schools and communities. I am doing the same thing now with corporations.

So, yes, of course this work will continue, but my colleagues and I at the Institute for Radical Forgiveness are also now committed to reducing the drop-off by extending that focus to include helping people not only maintain the high vibratory rate gained during the Radical Forgiveness experience, but to steadily increase it to as high a level as possible, so that there will be no going back. Also, to its becoming so integrated that it becomes part of who they are and what they do. To this end, we have instituted a wonderful new program called *Radical Empowerment.*

We call it this because, when we operate from a higher vibratory rate, our life changes very dramatically. Instead of always being the *effect* in a cause-and-effect world, we become the *cause* in our own life and in whatever we undertake as our life's calling. We are able to manifest what we want easily and quickly. We become truly empowered.

287

The focus of the Radical Empowerment program is YOU. It is a journey of self discovery. You will discover who you are in relation to others, to your purpose in life, and ultimately to Spirit. The goal is unconditional acceptance of, and deep appreciation for, who you are. That's Radical Empowerment.

One of the keys to this is also central to our maintaining our connection with the Radical Forgiveness vibration. I am referring to the systematic development of that part of our consciousness known as the *Observer*. This is the *self-aware* part of you that is able to witness or observe the whole community of selves within. From its vantage point outside of, or separate from you, it will, *if trained to do so*, notice when you begin to go unconscious. It will then take steps to bring you back — probably by reminding you to do the 4-Step process in that moment or listen to the 13 Steps. A trained Observer will keep you out of victimland, free and always at choice in your life.

Another question that inevitably comes up is: *"How can I effectively apply the Radical Forgiveness technology to every area of my life?*

The answer to this is also contained in the Radical Empowerment program which is, by the way, a mix of workshop experiences, on-line programs and tele-classes. Once you have integrated the Radical Forgiveness model into your consciousness and developed your Observer to a reasonably high degree, you will naturally begin to utilize Radical Forgiveness in every aspect of your life. It will be hard not to.

We will be supporting that in every possible way. For example as part of our Radical Empowerment program, we will be offering modules such as *Radical Parenting, Radical Weight Control, Radical Prosperity, Radical Relationships* and *Radical Health,* to name but a few. Keep your eyes on the web site for these programs coming into being.

The third question that always comes up once people simultaneously recognize, first, the potential of this work to make a huge difference in the world and, second, that in this work lies an opportunity for them to do meaningful and fulfilling spiritual work is: *"How can I share this with others so they can learn about this powerful work and receive the same benefits I have?"*

The answer is that we now have in place a professional certification program through which you can become trained to be a Radical Forgiveness Coach and Ceremony Facilitator. It is primarily a Home Study course, so it is very convenient and no previous qualifications are required. You will find details in Appendix II, on page 297, and on our web site.

Another way to respond to that question is by pointing out that Radical Forgiveness is a word of mouth phenomenon. Back in 1997, when I first published the book, I received a letter from the owner of one of the biggest independent bookstores in Atlanta. She said that she was noticing that people were coming in and buying a copy of the book and then returning a week or so later to buy six more for their friends. She wrote, "I have seen this phenomenon happen only with two other books, *Celestine Prophecy* and *Conversations With*

289

God, both of which have become best sellers. " I am not suggesting necessarily that you go out and buy six books to give away, but you would be contributing in a big way if you simply told your friends about Radical Forgiveness. There is probably no better way these days than to send out an e-mail message to everyone in your address book who you think might be interested. Thank you.

So there you have it — Radical Forgiveness is finally out of the closet. It has been, as it were, masquerading as simply a way to heal your life *(which, of course, it is),* but is now 'outed' as being a powerful technology that will, in addition to helping you heal and eradicate blocks in your life, raise your vibration considerably, awaken you fully and assist you in becoming an empowered spiritual being, fully able to shift easily between the third and fourth — and even the fifth dimensions of reality.

It is also a way for each of us, both individually and collectively, to make a significant difference in the world. As our vibratory rate increases, we will find ourselves being called to do more to help others and prepare for the great Awakening.

Thank you for being on this journey with me. There is much to look forward to and to be excited about, and I am grateful that you are in my life.

Namaste.

Colin Tipping   August 2003

Radical Forgiveness Workshops, Events and On-line Programs

Having now read the book — gift yourself the full Radical Forgiveness Experience by attending an event or taking an on-line program. Go to www.radicalforgiveness.com to check the schedule for the following opportunities.

• **The RF Ceremony:** Based on a Native American Healing Circle Ceremony, this 3-hour event enables people to forgive themselves and a whole host of others all at the same time. Since it is largely non-verbal, it is totally non-threatening.

• **The *Making Room for the Miracle* Workshop**. Friday evening and Saturday. A very practical, yet powerful and life-changing workshop that involves just the right amount of experiential work for newcomers to Radical Forgiveness.

• *Radical Awareness:* A great introduction to the RF technology; providing the opportunity to study the *Five Stages of Radical Forgiveness* in depth and to go through the *RF Worksheet,* and other processes, in detail, both cognitively and experientially. It can be done as an evening seminar over six weeks or as a one-and-a-half-day workshop.

• The *Miracles* **Workshop**. This weekend intensive is for those who want some 'hands-on' assistance and guidance from the facilitator in moving through deeply rooted forgiveness issues in a safe and loving space, with no more than 18 people participating. This incredible workshop will free you from the tyranny of the past, open the space for miracles to occur, completely alter your world-view, and change your life for the better in so many different ways. A truly transformational experience!

• The *Executive Miracles* **Workshop**
This exclusive, residential 'Miracles' workshop is designed specifically for high-profile people who need very special conditions, assuring them complete anonymity, security, privacy and confidentiality. For this workshop we use very carefully selected, high quality, secure venues.

• The *Emergence SELF* **Forgiveness Workshop**
A full weekend workshop in which people learn how to forgive themselves and find true self-acceptance, using the Radical Self Forgiveness technology.

• The *Circles of Forgiveness* **Workshop**
A one-day workshop that includes the RF ceremony as well as other powerful Radical Forgiveness processes. The straight 5-hour version is perfect for churches as a Sunday afternoon event. One of our most popular workshops.

• The *Radical Empowerment* **Series**
This is a combination of scheduled weekend, *in-person* workshops, on-line courses and tele-classes. The series is designed to help people to heal both the primal wounds of childhood and the associated toxic beliefs uncovered through the Radical Forgiveness experience. Also, to learn how to em-

power themselves by applying the Radical Forgiveness technology and the underlying philosophy, to every aspect of their lives, including prosperity, relationships, health, parenting, weight control, creativity, life purpose, etc.

• The Couples Retreat:
This is a powerful, residential retreat for couples who want to learn how to use the Radical Forgiveness technology to heal, or enhance, their relationship—or to move it towards a timely completion. Essential for any couple in a relationship crisis.

• Custom Designed Workshops For Business:
The application of this technology to any business organization increases productivity, raises morale, improves customer relations and boosts the bottom line. The effects are dramatic, long lasting and profound. (See page 296).

Special Workshops for the Clients of Professionals:
Psychotherapists, doctors and other professionals may wish to hire Colin Tipping or one of his highly trained staff to facilitate a special workshop exclusively for their clients.

Speaking Engagements:
Colin Tipping is available for lectures, keynote speaker engagements and private consultations. Call 770-428-9181.

FREE On-line Tutorial

While Chapter 20 gives all the necessary information on how to use the Radical Forgiveness Worksheet, a FREE tutorial is also available on our website, providing an online, interactive worksheet that will deepen your experience of the process. It is a wonderful enhancement to the book and we are happy to provide it at no charge. From the feedback that we have had, people just love it — and in many cases have preferred it to doing the worksheet on paper.

The program is very user-friendly and simple to use. It will take you, step-by-step, through the process of doing the worksheet to help you master the use of this extremely transformational tool.

It will be more meaningful to someone if they have read this book beforehand — Chapter 20 in particular. However, it is open and available to you, or anyone else, at any time and you can, of course, come back to it as many times as you wish. You might want to suggest to your friends that they try it too — even if they haven't yet read the book. To use the tutorial, go to.......

www.radicalforgiveness.com
At the Home page, click on 'Worksheet Tutorial'

The *On-line*
Radical Forgiveness Experience

Thanks to the great strides made in both teleconferencing and internet technology, the opportunity to experience all that the Radical Forgiveness technology has to offer, in the comfort of your own home no matter where you live in the world, is now here.

While the on-line experience is obviously quite different from attending a regular workshop, it is, in its own way, every bit as powerful and transformational. Check our web site, *www.radicalforgiveness.com* for an expanding number of interactive, on-line programs from which to choose, including one on **Self-forgiveness**, *(see chapter 30)*, and **Radical Empowerment,** *(see Afterword)*.

Some of them are **FREE**, such as the worksheet tutorial featured on the previous page and several of the programs associated with the "World Peace Through Radical Forgiveness Project," *(see pages 306 and 307)*. Others carry a fee.

The courses are designed to be either self-activated, instantly available programs that you just sign onto and do at your own pace, or as a scheduled course which is designed for an enrolled group working together over a definite period of time.

Isn't This Something! Radical Forgiveness Has
Now Become a Truly GLOBAL Experience

Radical Forgiveness in the Workplace

As we noted in the earlier chapters, our issues get triggered and subsequently acted out when we come into relationship with other people who mirror for us what we most need to heal. The workplace therefore offers the perfect environment for the creation of *healing dramas — and lots of them!*

Consequently, it follows that the workplace offers a great many opportunities for using Radical Forgiveness as an advanced form of conflict resolution and human energy management.

Conflicts and dramas cause energy blocks within the organization and we know that the Radical Forgiveness technology can be used to release them. Bearing in mind that a corporation will work best when energy *(in the form of money, information, materials and human energy),* is flowing easily and freely, it becomes obvious that the use of the RF technology, in some form acceptable to the corporate culture, will have a salutary effect on the bottom line, not to mention the improvement in morale.

I use the term Energy Management rather than Radical Forgiveness in the corporate setting and refer to the technology I have developed for corporations as **The Quantum Energy Management System,**™ or **'QEMS.'**™ for short. Look out for my book on the corporate connection coming out early in 2004

Appendix II

A Career In Radical Forgiveness Therapy & Coaching

The Institute for Radical Forgiveness Therapy and Coaching, Inc., was founded in 1998 by Colin Tipping to provide training and certification in Radical Forgiveness Therapy and Coaching. A subsidiary corporation was founded in Australia in October 2000 to do the same thing in that country.

The vision was — and still is — to train as many people as possible worldwide, to be able to articulate the principles of Radical Forgiveness to others in a simple and clear way so that more and more people have the opportunity to raise their vibration and shift their consciousness towards an alignment with spiritual principle. We see this as supporting the mission that we have accepted for ourselves, which is *"to raise the consciousness of the planet through the message of Radical Forgiveness."*

If you would like to join us in this joyful endeavor, whether you have previous qualifications or not, the opportunity to become trained and certified to take this message out to the world while helping people heal is available to you.

297

This will appeal to you if you have been searching for something to do that is spiritually more satisfying than your current work; or you are in the healing arts and would like to learn how to add a meaningful spiritual dimension to your work; or if you simply like helping people and feel drawn to do this work.

The Career Opportunity:

1. Radical Forgiveness Coach/Ceremony Facilitator:

Since it requires no prior professional training to become a Radical Forgiveness Coach and Ceremony Facilitator, this program represents a great opportunity for people without professional qualifications to learn how to provide help to others without crossing the line into doing what might traditionally be considered "therapy."

The Radical Forgiveness Coach is able to work one-on-one with people, to present short seminars; run the RF Ceremony; facilitate book study groups and run RF support groups.

2. RF Therapy Practitioner/Ceremony Facilitator:

The practitioner is also qualified to do all the above activities but, in addition, insofar as they have existing expertise and qualifications in recognized therapeutic modalities, such as psychotherapy, counseling, hypnotherapy, etc., they can add Radical Forgiveness to their own repertoire of healing modalities. However, the training is the same as for a Coach.

The opportunity to add this kind of spiritual dimension to their work is what many practitioners have been yearning for. The spiritual dimension is also what many clients are now seeking. People in need of help are increasingly turning only to those therapists who can offer it.

Post-Certification Training Opportunities

• On-line Program Coach
A Certified Ceremony Facilitator/RF Coach or Radical Forgiveness Therapy Practitioner may, after having reached a high level of expertise in RF coaching, apply to be trained as an on-line coach, associated with one or more of our on-line programs, as and when they become available.

• Radical Forgiveness Workshop Facilitator
A Certified Ceremony Facilitator/RF Coach or Radical Forgiveness Therapy Practitioner may, after having demonstrated to the Institute a proficiency in presentation and facilitation skills, will have the opportunity to apply to be trained as a facilitator of specific workshops, or groups of workshops.

• *Miracles* Workshop Facilitator
This advanced training is only available to Certified Radical Forgiveness Therapy Practitioners—i.e. those who are Board Certified Therapists with existing or potential facilitation skills.

• Life Coach
A Certified Ceremony Facilitator/RF Coach or Radical Forgiveness Therapy Practitioner may apply to take a course designed specifically for Certified RF Coaches by an associated Life Coach training school.

299

A Certification Training In Three Phases

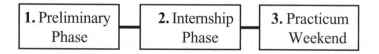

1. Preliminary Phase	2. Internship Phase	3. Practicum Weekend

Becoming certified as an RF Coach and Ceremony Facilitator is made easy by the fact that the first phase is a **Home Study Program**. There is no time limit on this phase and it is entirely up to you to decide when you are ready to begin the internship phase. The Home Study Kit contains a training manual, tapes, videos, books, CDs, etc. — everything you need to become fully educated about Radical Forgiveness and how it can be beneficially shared with people. *[In some cities, students form study groups and support each other through this phase]*.

2. During the **Internship Phase**, which must be completed within a 6 month period, you begin to put into practice, under supervision, what you have learned during the preliminary phase.

3. The Weekend Practicum may be taken during the 6-month internship or within a reasonable period afterwards, depending on where it might be taking place, difficulties with travel, etc. The idea is to bring together those who have been gathering on-the-job experience in order to compare notes, work collaboratively and refine their skills.

Further information about the professional training can be obtained from our web site *www.radicalforgiveness.com* or by calling **1-888-755-5696**.

Would You Like to Run a
Book Study Group?

Book study groups have sprung up all over the world— quite spontaneously it seems. Evidently, people bought the book and became so excited about it that they wanted to share it. They found a way to do that by getting people together and forming book study groups. Some do it in churches, bookstores, or even in their own homes.

FREE Guide:
To assist people in this we have produced a brief guide on how to run such a group. This is available as a download from our web site *www.radicalforgiveness.com.*

Becoming an Approved Book Study Facilitator Through Our Home-Study Program:
We have developed a more comprehensive home study program that you can take to become one of our Approved Radical Forgiveness Book Study Facilitators. This title is conferred by the Institute for Radical Forgiveness Therapy and Coaching, Inc. and entitles you to be on our approved list of Book Study Facilitators. You also receive the wholesaler's discount on the books. The cost of the Home Study Program is **$45**. *(Available on the web site).*

Radical Forgiveness
and Cancer

Since the connection between cancer and a marked inability to forgive is well established, you might think that forgiveness was the simple and logical answer to the problem. It never was, of course, but only because the only option was traditional forgiveness, and that took too long.

It's a very different situation with Radical Forgiveness. Because it is so quick, simple, easy to do and therapy free, Radical Forgiveness works. It is a great complementary treatment for cancer, MS, Chronic Fatigue and other immune system related diseases. *(The immune system is extremely susceptible to emotional stress — especially when it is suppressed or repressed).* It is very seldom that I do a Miracles workshop without one or two people in it who are journeying with cancer. I also consider that workshop to be my *cancer prevention* workshop.

Retreats
We also offer retreats in the North Georgia mountains at which people with any disease, but particularly with cancer, can receive profound healing of a spiritual nature, nurturing with good healthy food, and, through Radical Forgiveness, a gentle releasing of the stuck emotional energy that might have caused the problem in the first place. For more information go to the web site, *www.radicalforgiveness.com*

Appendix III

Additional Resources Available from our web site
www.radicalforgiveness.com

• AUDIO TAPES And CDs

i) The Radical Forgiveness Meditations
Side A: The Rose Forgiveness Meditation
Side B: A Wake For Your Wounded Inner Child

ii) Introduction to Radical Forgiveness
Side A: The Basics of Radical Forgiveness
Side B: The Proof of the Pudding

This tape outlines the essential principles of and the spiritual assumptions underlying Radical Forgiveness. It could easily be a life-line for you in moments of crisis. Play it as a reminder that, no matter how things look, you are exactly where you need to be and everything is in Divine order. On side B are some stories which are good reminders and interesting to share with people new to Radical Forgiveness. They are proof that it works.

iii) The *Satori* Grounding Meditation.
This tape by JoAnna Tipping gives a powerful meditation on how to become grounded and energetically balanced.

iv) The Book on Audio Tape:
Always an option for those who like to listen to tapes in the car. Enjoy Colin & his wife JoAnna reading the book together.

• VIDEOS:

i) Introduction to Radical Forgiveness:
A great adjunct to the book because even though the author is presenting the same concepts and ideas, you get the opportunity to hear it differently. Presented with warmth and charm you will find this video informative and useful. *(Appx 2hrs running time)*

ii) The Technology of Radical Forgiveness:
This is a video about how to use the tools and techniques that Radical Forgiveness provides. *(1hr)*

iii) Radical Relationships:
In this presentation, the author shows how we use relationships to heal ourselves and others. You will gain tremendous insight about the dynamics of relationships and how you can use Radical Forgiveness to improve them. *(1 hr)*

iv) Special Package:
Buy all three of the above videos for a special package price and save almost $15.00.

v) Cancer and Radical Forgiveness:
This video should be viewed by anyone who has cancer, has had cancer or is in any risk of getting cancer. It shows how important the emotional aspect is in the formation of cancer and shows how one can use Radical Forgiveness to prevent it. *(1hr)*

'Satori'

The Radical Forgiveness Game

The Radical Forgiveness Experience can be had in many different ways and I have described in this book most of the forms in which we have so far created it. This board game is the most recent and is, at the time of writing, in the process of being produced.

As you would expect, it takes you through the same five stages of Radical Forgiveness, but this time in the context of a game that can be played by up to five people and takes between 1-1/2 and 2 hours to play. It is a lot of fun but in the playing of it, energy is moved in the same mysterious way as it does in all the other forms of the Radical Forgiveness Experience.

We all pick a 'story' card to play with *(which invariably resonates a real situation for us)*, and we start in Victimland. We proceed around the board which spirals in towards the center, the objective being to reach the full Satori — the Awakening. We find ourselves picking up beliefs and energy blocks along the way, finding ways to release them or project them onto someone else. There are three Gateways to get through — the Gateway to Awareness; the Gateway to Shift Happens and the Gateway to Surrender. There is no winner or loser. The game ends when everyone reaches the Full Satori and joyfully reads out their reframe. *This game will be available early in 2004.*

Also by Colin Tipping:

'A RADICAL INCARNATION'

"The President of the United States Becomes Enlightened,
Heals America and Awakens Humanity —
A Spiritual Fantasy."

An inspiring story that, in addition to revealing profound spiritual truths, provides a Radical Forgiveness reframe for what appears to be happening in the world today and gives the means by which we each can make the vision of a healed and peaceful world a reality.

Accompany the soul of Jack Barber, a future President of the United States, as he is carefully tutored and prepared by Harley, his Senior Angel of Incarnation and Jeni, his Teacher-Angel, for his upcoming human experience on planet Earth.

Share his initial joy at having the opportunity to incarnate; his fascination with the concept of time; his incredulity when told about how humans behave and his frustration at learning that he will have no conscious memory of his own world — nor even of the lessons he is taking — once he is in a human body.

Be with him when he is shocked to learn that his mission is to become President in order to heal the soul of America and then lead all of Humanity towards its spiritual awakening — all to be achieved prior to 2012. Empathize with him as he agonizes over the enormity of his mission and learns the terrible consequences of his possible failure.

Be prepared also, to find yourself beginning to remember who you really are and becoming enrolled, by Harley, into holding the same vision as Jack — of a healed world and an awakened population ready to create Heaven-on-Earth in our time.

Published by Global 13 Publications, June 2003. $14.95
Available in Bookstores or from *www.radicalforgiveness.com*

The *'Harley's Angels'* Club

"Harley's Angels," is a virtual club composed of people willing to hold the vision and the intention of creating World Peace and a World of Forgiveness by 2012.

The members are mostly people who have read my book, *'A Radical Incarnation'* (see page 306), and who have heeded the call to participate in the *'World Peace Through Radical Forgiveness Project,'* the objectives of which are, firstly, to heal the soul of America and, secondly, to awaken Humanity to itself. We have the technology to do it; all we need is a few thousand people—like you—to take a little bit of time to go to the web site, click on **America's Healing** and then do one or more of the on-line worksheets to be found there.

You might be wondering how that could possibly make a difference to an idea that big? Well, since reality is holographic in nature, when any one of us makes a shift in our own energy field (consciousness), the effect is felt throughout the entire collective energy field of humanity. That's why when we do something to raise our own consciousness, we raise the consciousness of humanity and contribute to its awakening. Your individual contribution therefore is extremely valuable. A relatively small number of people holding a similar vibration can literally change the world.

To get the full picture, read *A Radical Incarnation* and then go the web site and click on *America's Healing*. Find out for yourself how we can heal this country's shadow, easily and quickly, and create the conditions for Humanity's Awakening.

The 13 Steps

Sometimes the written word simply isn't enough. There are some things that just have to be heard. *The 13 Step Process is one of those.* Just reading it would have very little effect I feel, so rather than put it in the book I have chosen to make it available to you in its most potent form — as a recording. I give an introduction, of course, and then ask you 13 questions to which you simply answer 'Yes.' That's it! It's so simple you can't imagine that it could change anything, but it does. Debi's story in Chapter 16 is evidence of this. *(We feature one of Debi's own songs on the CD.)*

The are also four songs featuring our very own **Karen Taylor-Good.** Her work is so wonderful and so in alignment with Radical Forgiveness, it's like she is part of every workshop we do — if not in person then on CDs and tapes. You will simply love these four songs. If you want more — come to our website for a selection of her CDs.

We are making this recording available to you on CD at the price of **$13.00** + S & H. It's the most valuable recording you will ever own. It will almost certainly improve your relationships — and perhaps even save your life!

Don't delay - order today!

www.radicalforgiveness.com or 1-888-755-5696